DOLLY ALDERTON

Biography

Everything I've Learned About Love

and Growing Up

CONTENT

EVERYTHING I KNEW ABOUT LOVE AS A TEENAGER

Romantic love is the most significant and fascinating thing in the universe.

If you don't have it when you're an adult, you've failed, just like so many of my art professors, who are 'Miss' instead of 'Mrs', have frizzy hair, and wear ethnic jewelry.

It is vital to have a large number of sexual encounters, but no more than ten.

When I'm a single woman in London, I'll be really stylish and skinny, wearing black dresses and drinking Martinis, and only meeting men at book releases and exhibition openings.

When two boys fight physically over you, you know you've found true love. The sweet spot is bleeding, but no one needs to go to the hospital. If I am lucky, this will happen to me someday.

It is critical to lose your virginity after the seventeenth birthday but before the eighteenth birthday. Even if it was only the day before, you will never have sex if you remain a virgin until your seventeenth year. You can snog as many people as you like, it doesn't matter; it's simply practice.

The coolest boys are always tall, Jewish, and own cars.

Older lads are the best kind since they are more sophisticated and worldly, and they have slightly lower standards.

When friends have lovers, they get uninteresting. A friend having a boyfriend is only fun if you also have a boyfriend.

If you never question your friend about their guy, they'll eventually figure out that you find it uninteresting and quit talking about him.

It's an excellent idea to get married later in life, after you've lived a while. Say, twenty-seven.

Farly and I will never be interested in the same boy because she prefers them short and cheeky, like Nigel Harman, while I prefer them macho and mysterious, like Busted's Charlie Simpson. This is why our friendship will endure forever.

No moment in my life will ever be as romantic as when Lauren and I were playing that weird pub in St Albans on Valentine's Day and I sang 'Lover, You Should've Come Over,' and Joe Sawyer sat at the front and closed his eyes because we'd just talked about Jeff Buckley, and he's the only boy I've ever met who completely understands me and where I'm coming from.

No event in my life will ever be as embarrassing as when I tried to kiss Sam Leeman and he pulled away, causing me to fall over.

No moment in my life has ever been more sad than when Will Young came out as gay and I had to pretend I was fine with it, but I cried as I burnt the leather book I was given for my confirmation, in which I had written about our life together.

Boys enjoy it when you say unpleasant things to them, and they think being too nice is childish and uncool.

When I eventually find a boyfriend, little else will matter.

BOYS

Some people associate their adolescence with the happy shrieks of their siblings playing in the garden. Others heard the chain rattle of their beloved bike as they hobbled along hills and valleys. Some will recall hearing birdsong on their way to school, or the sound of laughter and footballs being kicked in the playground. For me, it sounded like AOL dial-up internet.

I can still recall it, note by note. The tinny initial phone beeps, the reedy, half-finished squiggles of sound that signaled a half-connection, the high one note that indicated progress, followed by two abrasive low thumps and some white fuzz. The silence showed that you had overcome the worst of it. 'Welcome to AOL,' murmured a calming voice with an upward accent on the 'O'. followed by, 'You have email.' I'd dance around the room to the sound of the AOL dial-up to pass the time. I choreographed a dance using techniques I learned in ballet: a plié on the beeps and a pas de chat on the thumps. I did that every night after I got home from school. Because that was the music for my life. Because I spent my adolescence using the internet.

A little explanation: I grew up in the suburbs. That's the explanation. When I was eight years old, my parents made the awful decision to relocate us from a basement flat in Islington to a larger property in Stanmore, which is the last stop on the Jubilee line and on the outskirts of North London. It was the city's blank margin; an observer of the joy rather than a participant in the party.

Growing up in Stanmore, you are neither urban nor rural. I was too far from London to be one of those cool kids that went to the Ministry of Sound and dropped their 'g's while wearing nice vintage clothes from the surprisingly good Oxfam in Peckham Rye. But I was too far away from the Chilterns to be one of those ruddy-cheeked, feral, country youths who wore old fisherman's jumpers and learned how to drive their father's Citroën when they were thirteen. They went on hikes and took acid in a forest with their relatives. The North London suburbs lacked an identity. It was beige, just like the luxurious carpeting that graced every home. There was no art, no culture, no historic structures, no parks, and no independent stores or restaurants. There were golf courses, Prezzo branches, private schools, driveways, roundabouts, retail parks, and glass-roofed shopping malls. The women all looked the same, the buildings were built the same way, and the cars were all identical. The only way to express oneself was to spend money on homogenized assets such as conservatories, kitchen expansions, automobiles with built-in satnav, and all-inclusive trips to Mallorca. There was nothing to do but play golf, have your hair highlighted, or peruse a Volkswagen showroom.

This was especially true if you were a teenager who relied on your mother's availability to transport you in the aforementioned Volkswagen Golf GTI. Fortunately, I had my best buddy, Farly, who lived a three-and-a-half-mile bike ride away from my cul de sac.

Farly was, and still is, unlike any other individual in my life. We met at school when we were 11 years old. She was and still is diametrically opposed to me. She is black, but I am fair. She is a little short, and I am a touch too tall. She planned and schedules everything; I leave things till the last minute. She enjoys order, but I prefer disorder. She adores regulations; I despise rules. She has no ego; I believe my morning toast is important enough to be aired across three social media channels. She is very present and focused on the task at hand, whereas I am constantly half in life and half in a fanciful version of it in my imagination. But somehow, we make it work. Nothing has been luckier in my life than the day Farly sat next to me in a math class in 1999.

Farly's daily routine was always the same: we'd sit in front of the television, eating mountains of bagels and crisps (though only when our parents were away - another characteristic of the suburban middle class is that they are particularly precious about sofas and always have a 'strictly no eating' living room), and watching American teen sitcoms on Nickelodeon. When we'd finished watching Sister, Sister, Two of a Kind, and Sabrina the Teenage Witch, we'd go to the music channels, staring slack-jawed at the screen and clicking between MTV, MTV Base, and VH1 every ten seconds in search of a certain Usher video. When we got bored, we'd go back to Nickelodeon + 1 and watch all of the episodes of the American teen sitcoms we'd seen an hour before, on repeat.

Morrissey famously described his adolescent life as 'waiting for a bus that never came', a sense that's only worsened when you reach adulthood in a setting that feels like a bland waiting room. I was bored, miserable, and lonely, desperately wishing the hours of my childhood away. Then, like a noble knight in shining armor, AOL dial-up internet appeared on my family's enormous desktop computer. Then came MSN Instant Messenger.

When I downloaded MSN Messenger and began adding email address connections - friends from school, friends of friends, and friends from adjacent schools whom I'd never met - it felt like knocking on the wall of a prison cell and hearing someone respond. It was like discovering blades of grass on Mars. It was like turning on the radio and eventually hearing the crackling transition into a real voice. It was an escape from my suburban drudgery and into a plethora of human activity.

As a teenager, MSN was more than just a tool for me to communicate with my pals; it was also a place. That's how I remember it, as a room where I sat for hours and hours every evening and weekend, staring at the television until my eyes went bloodshot. Even when we left the suburbs and my parents generously took my brother and me on vacation in France, it was still the room I occupied every day. When we arrived at a new B&B, the first thing I did was check to see if they had an internet-connected computer - usually an ancient desktop in a dark basement - and then I would log on to MSN Messenger and unashamedly chat on it for hours while a moody French teenager sat behind me in an armchair waiting for his turn. The Provençal sun beat down outside, as the rest of my family read by the pool, but my parents understood there was no debating with me about MSN Messenger. It was the center of all of my friendships. It was my own personal space. It was the only possession I could call my own. As I mentioned, it was a location.

My first email address, munchkin_1_4@hotmail.com, was created when I was twelve years old at my school's IT room. I chose the number 14 because I figured I'd only be emailing for two years before it became childish; I gave myself enough time to enjoy this new fad and its different idiosyncrasies before the address became obsolete on my fourteenth birthday. I didn't start using MSN Messenger until I was fourteen, and around that time, I experimented using willyoungisyum@hotmail.com to show my newfound love for Pop Idol's 2002 champion. I also attempted thespian_me@hotmail.com on after delivering a barnstorming performance as Mister Snow in the school's Carousel production.

When I downloaded MSN Instant Messenger, I returned to munchkin_1_4 and loved the enormous MSN Messenger contacts book of school buddies I had amassed since the address's inception. However, there was also the introduction of boys. I didn't know any boys by this stage. Except for my brother, small cousin, father, and one or two of my father's cricketing pals, I had never spent time with a boy in my life. But MSN provided the email addresses and avatars of these new floating Phantom Boys, which were generously contributed by various females at my school - the ones who would hang out with boys on weekends and then graciously distribute their email addresses around the student body. These boys dominated the MSN circuit; every female at my school would add them as a contact, and we'd all have our fifteen minutes of fame talking to them.

The boys were sourced from three general categories. The first was a girl's mother's godson or a distant family friend with whom she had grown up. He was usually a year or two older than us, quite tall and lean, with a deep voice. This category also included someone's schoolboy neighbour. The next level of classification included someone's cousins or second cousins. Finally, and most exotically, someone met a boy while on a family vacation. This was the Holy Grail, really, because he might be anywhere, as far away as Bromley or Maidenhead, and you'd be talking to him on MSN Messenger as if he were right there. What crazy, what adventure.

I soon compiled a Rolodex of these waifs and strays, labeling them 'BOYS' in my contacts list. Weeks would pass conversing with them about GCSE choices, favorite songs, how much we smoked and drank, and 'how far' we'd 'been' with the opposite sex (always a laborious work of fabrication). Of course, we had little to no idea what someone looked like; this was before camera phones and social media profiles, so all you had to go on was their little MSN profile photo and self-description. Sometimes I'd go to the bother of using my mother's scanner to upload an image of me looking great at a family meal or on vacation, and then I'd carefully crop out my aunt or grandfather using Paint's crop tool, but it was usually too much of a hassle.

The introduction of virtual lads into the lives of our schoolmates brought with it a slew of new tensions and drama. There would be a never-ending rumour mill about who was speaking to whom. Girls would swear their trust to boys they'd never met by entering the boy's first name into their username and adding stars, hearts, and underscores on either side. Some girls thought they were in an intimate online conversation with a boy, but the usernames that popped up told a different story. Sometimes, girls from neighboring schools who you'd never met would add you and ask if you were talking to the same boy they were. Occasionally, and this would always be remembered as a cautionary story in the common room, you might accidently reveal an MSN relationship with a boy by writing a message to him in the wrong window and sending it to a buddy instead. Tragedies like to Shakespeare's would ensue.

There was a complicated etiquette that came with MSN; if both you and a boy you liked were logged on but he wasn't talking to you, a failsafe way to get his attention would be to log off and then log back on, as he would be notified of your re-entry and reminded of your presence, hopefully resulting in a conversation. There was also the option of disguising your online status if you wanted to avoid communicating to anyone other than a specific contact, which you could do discreetly. It was a complicated Edwardian courtship dance, and I was ecstatic and eager to participate.

These lengthy correspondences rarely culminated in a real-life meeting, and when they did, it was almost always a crushing disappointment. There was Max with the double-barrelled surname, a legendary MSN Casanova known for sending girls Baby G watches in the mail, and Farly arranged to meet outside a newsagent in Bushey one Saturday afternoon after months of conversing online. She arrived, took one glance at him, and ran behind a trashcan to hide. She watched him repeatedly call her phone from a phone box, but she couldn't bear the thought of meeting him in person and fled home. They continued to talk for hours every night on MSN.

I had two. The first was an unsuccessful blind date at a shopping mall that lasted less than fifteen minutes. The second was a boy from a local boarding school who I had communicated with for over a year before our first meeting at Pizza Express in Stanmore. For the next year, we had an on-and-off relationship, primarily because he was constantly locked up at school. But I'd go to see him on occasion, dressed in lipstick and carrying a handbag full of packets of cigarettes I'd bought for him, much like Bob Hope was sent out to entertain the troops during WWII. He didn't have internet access in his dormitory, so MSN wasn't an option, but we made up for it with weekly letters and long phone calls that made my father cry when he received a three-figure monthly telephone bill.

When I was fifteen, I began a love affair more intense than anything I had ever experienced in the windows of MSN Instant Messenger when I met Lauren, a wild-haired girl with freckles and kohl-rimmed hazel eyes. We'd seen each other at the occasional Hollywood Bowl birthday party since we were youngsters, but we finally met in person through our mutual friend Jess over dinner at one of Stanmore's many Italian chain restaurants. The connection was similar to anything I'd seen in a romantic film on ITV2. We chatted until our jaws were dry, finished each other's words, and made tables turn as we laughed like drains; Jess went home, and we waited on a bench in the bitter cold after being kicked out of the restaurant just to keep talking.

She was a guitarist searching for a singer to form a band; I'd performed at a little open-mic event in Hoxton and wanted a guitar. We began rehearsing bossa nova renditions of Dead Kennedys songs the next day in her mother's shed, with the first draft of our band name being 'Raging Pankhurst'. We eventually altered it to the much more bizarre 'Sophie Can't Fly'. Our first gig was at a Turkish restaurant in Pinner, where there was just one other client who wasn't a family member or a school buddy. We went on to undertake all the big names, including a theater foyer in Rickmansworth, a dilapidated outbuilding in Mill Hill's bar garden, and a cricket pavilion just outside Cheltenham. We busked on any street without a police officer. We sang at the reception for any bar mitzvah that invited us.

We also had a passion for the innovative way of multi-platforming our MSN content. Early in our acquaintance, we learned that, since the inception of Instant Messenger, we had both been copying and pasting discussions with boys onto a Microsoft Word document, printing them, and storing the pages in a ring-binder folder to read before bed like an erotic novel. We considered ourselves to be a two-person Bloomsbury Group of early 2000s MSN Messenger.

But, just as I was developing a friendship with Lauren, I left suburban life to attend a co-ed boarding school 75 miles north of Stanmore. MSN could no longer satisfy my curiosity about the opposite sex; I wanted to know what they were like in real life. The ever-fading scent of Ralph Lauren Polo Blue on a love letter didn't satisfy me anymore, nor did the pings and drums of fresh messages on MSN. I went to boarding school to try to get used to boys.

(Aside: Thank God, I did. Farly continued for sixth form at our all-girls school, and when she arrived at university, having never spent any time with boys, she was like an uncut bull in a china shop. On the first night of freshers' week, there was a 'traffic light party' where single people were urged to wear something green and couples to wear something red. Most of us assumed this meant a green T-shirt, but Farly appeared to our halls of residence bar dressed in green tights, green shoes, a green dress, and a large green bow in her hair, complete with a mist of green hairspray. She could as well have had I WENT TO AN ALL-GIRLS SCHOOL tattooed across her forehead. I am eternally pleased that I spent two years on the nursery slopes of mixed contact at boarding school; otherwise, I worry I might have fallen foul of the can of green hairspray come freshers' week.

As it turned out, I learned that I had nothing in common with most boys and had little interest in them save for the desire to kiss them. And no male I wanted to kiss wanted to kiss me, so I could have stayed in Stanmore and continued to enjoy a series of dream partnerships that took place in the fertile areas of my mind.

I attribute my high expectations for love to two factors: the first is that I am the kid of parents who are almost shamefully smitten with each other, and the second is the films I watched in my early years. As a child, I had a unique love with vintage musicals, and having grown up seeing Gene Kelly and Rock Hudson films, I expected boys to carry themselves with the same elegance and charm. However, co-ed schools quickly dispelled this misconception. Consider my first politics lesson. I was one of only two girls in the class of twelve, and I'd never sat with so many boys in one room in my life. The most attractive lad, who I had already been told was a known heartthrob (his older brother, who had gone the year before, was dubbed 'Zeus'), passed a piece of paper to me down the table as our teacher described what Proportional Representation was. The message was wrapped up and had a heart painted on the front, so I assumed it was a love letter; I opened it with a cheeky smile. However, as I unfolded it, there was an image of a creature, kindly annotated to tell me that it was an orc from Lord of the Rings, with 'YOU LOOK LIKE THIS' scrawled underneath it.

Farly came to see me on weekends and ogled at the hundreds of boys of various shapes and sizes strolling the streets with sports bags and hockey sticks slung over their shoulder. She couldn't believe how lucky I was to be able to sit in pews in church every morning within reach of them. However, I found the reality of boys to be little disappointing. Not as hilarious as the girls I met there, and not nearly as interesting or friendly. And, for some reason, I could never really relax around any of them.

By the time I left school, I had ceased using MSN Messenger as much as I used to. My first term at Exeter University ended, and with it came the introduction of Facebook. Facebook was a treasure trove for lads online, and this time, even better, you could find all of their important information on one page. I would constantly scroll through my uni friends' photos and add anyone who I liked the look of; this would swiftly escalate into messages back and forth and scheduled meet-ups at one of the several Vodka Shark club nights or foam parties taking place that week. I was at a campus university in a cathedral city in Devon; we had no trouble finding one other. If MSN was a blank canvas on which I could paint wild dreams, Facebook messaging was only a functional meet-up tool. It was how students determined their next victory and planned their next Thursday night.

By the time I finished university and moved to London, I had completely abandoned my practice of cold-calling potential love prospects on Facebook with the persuasive aggression of an Avon representative, but a new pattern was emerging. I would meet a man through a friend, at a party, or on a night out, acquire his name and phone number, and then build an epistolary connection with him via text or email for weeks and weeks before agreeing to a second real-life meeting. Perhaps it was because this was the only way I'd learned to get to know someone, with a distance between us and enough space for me to curate and filter the best version of myself possible - all the good jokes, all the best sentences, all the songs I knew he'd like, usually sent to me by Lauren. In exchange, I would send her songs to pass along to her pen buddy. She once said that we transmitted good new music to each other at wholesale prices and then passed it on to love partners as our own, with a 'emotional mark-up'.

This type of correspondence nearly invariably resulted in disappointment. I gradually realized that it is preferable for first dates to take place in person rather than in writing; otherwise, the gap between who you envision the other person to be and who they actually are grows larger and wider. Many times, I would imagine a person and our chemistry as if I were writing a screenplay, only to be crushed when we met again in real life. It was as if, when things didn't go as planned, I expected he'd been given a copy of the screenplay I'd written, and I'd be irritated that his agency had apparently forgotten to courier it to him to memorize.

Any woman who spent her early years surrounded solely by other girls would tell you the same thing: you never get over the notion that boys are the most interesting, alluring, repugnant, weird creatures to roam the globe; as deadly and legendary as a Sasquatch. Most of the time, it also signifies you're a lifelong fantasy enthusiast. Why wouldn't you be? For years, all I did was sit on walls with Farly, kicking the bricks with my thick rubber soles and staring up at the sky, trying to come up with something to divert us from the never-ending sight of hundreds of girls wandering about us in matching uniform. When you attend an all-girls school, your imagination gets a daily exercise like an Olympic athlete's. It's remarkable how accustomed you become to the burning fire of fantasy when you retreat to it so frequently.

I always assumed that my fascination and fixation with the opposite sex would fade as soon as I left school and began my life, but little did I know that in my late twenties, I would be as naive about how to interact with them as I was when I first logged on to MSN.

Boys were problematic. One that would take me 15 years to repair.

THE BAD DATE DIARIES: TWELVE MINUTES

The year is 2002. I am 14 years old. I'm wearing a Miss Selfridge kilt skirt, black Dr Martens, and a neon orange crop top.

The boy is Betzalel, a friend of Natalie's from school. They met at a

Jewish holiday camp and have been talking on MSN and giving each other'relationship and life advise' since. Natalie is looking for new friends after losing hers by circulating rumors that a girl in our year is self-harming when it is actually bad eczema, and I am one of her targets.

She knows I desire a boyfriend, so she proposes connecting Betz and me on MSN Messenger. I am quite content with the implicit deal that Natalie gives me a new boy to talk to in exchange for the occasional lunch with her.

Betz and I are basically splitting up after a month of talking every day after school on MSN. He, like me, considers everyone his age to be immature, and he, too, is tall for his age. We are continually chewing the fat from our common experiences.

We agree to meet at Costa at Brent Cross Shopping Centre. I invite Farly to join me so that I am not alone.

Betz arrives, and he looks nothing like the photo he sent me; he has shaved off all of his curly hair and gained a lot of weight since camp. We wave across the table. Betz places no orders.

Farly does all the talking, while Betz and I look at the floor, humiliated and silent. Betz has a shopping bag and tells us he just got Toy Story 2 on video. I tell him that's childish. He claims my skirt makes me look like a Scottish man.

I tell him we must leave because we need to catch the 142 back to Stanmore. The date lasts for twelve minutes.

When I get home and log on to MSN, Betz instantly sends me a lengthy message that I know he has already written in Microsoft Word and copied and pasted into the chat window in his distinctive italic purple Comic Sans. He says he thinks I am a nice girl, but he has no affections for me. I tell him it's inappropriate for him to make a speech and sit at home waiting for me to log on when he lives so close to Brent Cross and my bus is twenty-five minutes away, simply because he knew I fancied him less than he fancied me and didn't want me to say it first.

Betz blocks me for a month, but eventually forgives me. We never meet again, yet we become confidants until I am seventeen.

Natalie and I will never eat lunch together again now that I am free of my contractual obligations.

THE BAD PARTY CHRONICLES: UCL HALLS, NEW YEAR'S EVE, 2006

It's my first vacation home after my first term of university. Lauren, who is also home for Christmas, advises that we attend a New Year's Eve party in the UCL halls of residence. She's been invited by Hayley, a schoolmate she hasn't seen since prize-giving.

We arrive at the enormous common flat in a rundown building located on a backstreet between Euston and Warren Streets. The partygoers include a diverse group of UCL stoners, Lauren's school mates, and opportunistic passers-by who see the door open and hear R. Kelly's 'Ignition' on repeat for the majority of the evening. Lauren and I each have a bottle of red wine (Jacob's Creek Shiraz, because it's a special occasion), and we drink it from two plastic glasses.

I check the room for lads with functional limbs and a discernible heartbeat. At this moment, I am eighteen and six months into my sexually active life and at a highly heightened stage of libido; an ephemeral phase in which sex was my greatest adventure and discovery; a time when shagging was as common as potatoes and tobacco, and I am Sir Walter Raleigh. I couldn't understand why people weren't doing it all the time. All the novels, films, and songs written about it were insufficient to describe all aspects of how wonderful it was; how could anyone perceive an opportunity in any evening for anything other than having sex or finding someone to have sex with? (This emotion had gradually faded by my eighteenth birthday.)

I saw a familiar, welcoming face on a tall physique with broad shoulders and recognize him as the runner on a comedy where I did work experience after completing my GCSE exams. We'd flirt and gossip about the diva cast members while smoking cigarettes behind the studio. We approach each other with outstretched arms for hugs and almost immediately begin snogging. This is how I behaved when my hormones were coursing through my system so quickly; a handshake became a snog, and a hug became a dry hump. The social markers of intimacy all moved up a few steps.

After a few hours of sharing Shiraz and rubbing up against each other, we lock ourselves in the toilet to complete the transaction. We are fumbling with each other's slacks and skirts, intoxicated teens attempting to repair a damaged fuse box, when there is a knock at the door.

'THE LOO IS NOT WORKING!' I yell, The Runner chewing on my neck.

'Doll,' Lauren hisses. 'It's me; allow me in.' I button up my skirt, approach to the door, and open it slightly.

'What?' I ask, sticking my head around. She moves in through the gap. 'So I've been getting off with Finn—' She spots my pal in the corner of the restroom, awkwardly zipping up his jeans. 'Oh, hello,' she says to him casually. 'So I'm getting off with Finn, but I'm terrified he'll feel my knickers.'

'So?'

'They're control trousers,' she explains, raising her garment to reveal a flesh-colored girdle. 'To keep your stomach and back fat in.'

'So, just take them off. 'Pretend you weren't wearing any,' I say, pushing her toward the door.

'Where should I place them? Everyone is in every room; I've been in every room, and there are groups in each one.

"Put them there," I reply, pointing behind the loo's dirty cistern. 'Nobody will locate them.' I help Lauren pull them down her legs, stuff them behind the loo, and push her out.

Unfortunately, The Runner is unable to perform owing to the copious amounts of booze consumed and the shared spliff. We make many attempts to fix the situation, one of which is so frantic that we accidently unhinge the shower unit from the wall, but none of them are successful. So we cut our losses and parted ways peacefully; he leaves for another party, and we embrace farewell. It has just passed midnight.

Lauren and I meet in the room where the most marijuana is smoked to catch up on our different veneries. Finn has also left for the promise of a better celebration in the darkest first hours of the new year. We salute the effectiveness of friendship and the never-ending disappointment of boys before spotting and quickly befriending an emo band we met on the Whetstone open-mic circuit. She selects the vocalist with Robert Smith hair, and I take the bassist with Cabbage Patch Doll cheeks. We all lean against a wardrobe, handing Silk Cuts and spliffs up and down our four-person factory line and taking turns inserting our iPods into the speaker dock to play an even mix of John Mayer and Panic! At the disco. The music abruptly ceases.

'Someone has broken the shower,' Hayley says imperiously. 'We need to discover the guy who broke the shower because they must pay for it, otherwise we'll get in big problems with the warden.'

'Yes, we need to find them,' I say with a slur. 'I believe it was the short guy with long hair.'

'Which guy?'

I say, "He was here a moment ago." 'It was definitely him; he emerged from the bathroom with a girl and they were laughing. I believe he went outside to smoke a cigarette.

I lead a witch-hunt of the halls' residents out onto the street to find the bogus man, but I quickly lose interest in the ruse when I meet Joel, who is searching for the party. Joel is a well-known North London heartthrob, a Jewish Warren Beatty with gelled spikes and acne scars—the suburbs' Danny Zuko. I offer him a cigarette, and we start snogging as if we were exchanging small chat about TFL. We return to the apartment, where I enjoy publicly snogging Joel, a few kudos points higher than The Runner of yesteryear. I'm simply disappointed that I won't be able to occupy the bathroom again, which is now busy with Hayley and her half-baked Silent Witness squad of party-pooper forensics attempting to determine who broke the shower and how. Christine, a lovely blonde (the Sandy to Joel's Danny), approaches me as I am hunting for a new hiding place. I cheerfully leave them to it because, as the saying goes, "If you want to shag something, let it go."

Lauren and I regroup for a cigarette before heading to the Mayfairs.

'They used to go out when we were at school,' she explains. "Very up and down, very intense."

'Oh,' I respond.

I look across the room and see Christine and Joel holding hands as they leave the flat. He apologizes and waves at me as he leaves.

He mouthed 'bye'.

Lauren is concerned with the emo singer, and they are discussing chord progressions, which is a sure sign that she is dedicated to the concept of sex. It is nearly four a.m., and I need to wake up in two hours to get to my job as a sales assistant at an exclusive Bond Street shoe shop, where I am paid a one percent commission that I cannot afford to lose. I hunt for a piece of carpet to sleep on in a gloomy room and, to my pleasure, locate an unoccupied single bed. I set my alarm for six a.m.

Two hours later, I wake up with the worst hangover I've ever had; my head feels like it's been turned inside out, my eyes are glued together with mascara, and my breath smells like a Sauvignon-swilling rat crept into my mouth during the night and died and decayed. I stare down at my brown Topshop miniskirt, bare legs, and pirate boots, recalling that I did not have my work uniform with me.

'Hayley,' I hiss, nudging her body with my big toe while she sleeps on a pile of jumpers on the floor beside me. 'Hayley. I need to borrow a dress. Just a regular black dress. I'll return it later today.'

'You're in my bed,' she states plainly. 'You wouldn't come out of it last night.'

'Sorry,' I respond.

'And Lauren told me you broke the shower,' she murmurs into the sweaters. I say nothing, leave quietly, and regret the altruism I demonstrated only a few hours before by discovering a notebook of Hayley's sad little poetry under her pillow and not reading it from cover to cover.

'You look like a homeless person,' my witchy-faced boss Mary snarls as I enter the office. 'You smell like one, too. "Get down to the stockroom," she replies dismissively, sweeping her hand at me as if batting away a fly. 'You cannot be around consumers today.'

When I come home that night, after the longest day of work in my life, I log on to Facebook to assess the picture damage from the previous night. At the top of my webpage, Hayley has posted a close-up shot of Lauren's large knickers into an album labeled 'Lost Property'. Everyone at the gathering gets tagged. The caption merely says, 'Whose pants are these?'

A HELLRAISER HEADS TO LEAMINGTON SPA

I was ten years old when I became intoxicated for the first time. I attended Natasha Bratt's bat mitzvah, along with four other lucky chosen girls from our year. In the sun-drenched marquee in their Mill Hill back garden, the wine flowed and the smoked salmon circled; the women's hair was blow-dried into violently undulating trajectories, their lips a uniform frosted beige. And for reasons I'll never understand, the catering staff served glass after glass of champagne to all of us girls, who were clearly prepubescent in our Tammy Girl strapless dresses and butterfly clips in our hair.

At first, it seemed like a wave of warmth rushing through my body, my blood racing and my epidermis buzzing. Then it was as if all the screws in my joints had been removed, leaving me as springy and light as freshly made dough. Then came the chatting: amusing stories, theatrical impressions of instructors and parents, harsh jokes, and the greatest swear words. (To this day, this three-step progression still describes my initial drunkenness.)

The father-daughter dance to Van Morrison's 'Brown Eyed Girl' came to an abrupt and premature end when one of the girls, slightly further along than the rest of us, threw herself belly-first on the dance floor and wiggled manically underneath the legs of both parties, like a flapping fish out of water. I swiftly followed suit before we were both removed and chastised by an irate uncle. But the night had only just started.

Flooded with newfound confidence, I decided it was time for my first kiss, then my second (his closest friend), and finally my third (the first's brother). Everyone got involved, switching and experimenting with kissing partners as if they were shared puddings at a table. Eventually, this suburban child organization was disbanded, and we were all ushered to the front room and served black coffee; the door was locked, and our parents were summoned to collect us. The bad behavior was so out of the ordinary that our headmistress reprimanded us a second time on Monday, accusing us of'representing the school in a bad light'.

I was never the same after that night, the events of which gave ample fodder to fill the pages of my diaries long into my teen years. At far too young an age, I developed a taste for booze. I asked for little, diluted glasses of wine at all family gatherings. At Christmas, I'd slurp the delicious, throat-catching liquid from the guts of liqueur chocolates, hoping for a hit. At fourteen, I discovered where my parents kept the key to their drinks cupboard and would drink capfuls of cheap French brandy while they were away, relishing the warm, dizzy cloud it cast over homework. Sometimes I'd entice Farly to join me on a secret suburban binge; we'd guzzle their Beefeater gin and refill it with water, then sit cross-legged on the plush carpet and watch Who Wants to Be a Millionaire?, drunkenly squabbling over the correct answer.

I've never despised anything more than being a teenager. I couldn't have been more unsuited to adolescence. I was desperate to be an adult and to be regarded seriously. I despised relying on others for anything. I'd rather clean floors than be handed pocket money, or walk three miles in the rain at night than be driven home by a parent. When I was fifteen, I looked up the cost of one-bedroom flats in Camden so that I could start saving with my babysitting money. At the same age, I was hosting 'dinner parties' with my mother's recipes and dining table, forcing my friends to come over for rosemary roast chicken tagliatelle and raspberry pavlovas with a Frank Sinatra soundtrack when all they wanted to do was eat burgers and go bowling. I wanted to have my own friends, schedule, home, money, and life. Being a teenager was a huge, irritating, mortifying, exposing, co-dependent disgrace that I couldn't wait to get over.

Alcohol, I believe, was my modest form of independence. It was the only way I could feel like an adult. All of my friends' drinking-related activities, such as snogging, shrieking, secret-swapping, smoking, and dancing, were enjoyable, but it was the relevant adultness of booze that I preferred. I would act out fictitious scenes from everyday adulthood. I would confidently walk into local off-licences and explore the backs of bottles while pretending to talk into my Nokia 3310 about 'a casual drinks party on Saturday', 'a nightmare day in the office', or 'where I left the car'. While holding my dog-eared copy of The Female Eunuch (ironically, mainly decorative), I would place myself in the middle of the corridor within earshot of teachers in the four o'clock rush out of school on a Friday and shout, 'WE'RE STILL ON FOR DINNER, YEAH?' at Farly, 'I FANCY A FULL-BODIED BOTTLE OF RED!' and enjoy the slightly perplexed look on their faces as they passed me. Well, screw you, I would say. I'm doing something you do, too. I am drinking. I am an adult. Take me fucking serious.

I didn't really develop a hard drinking habit until I went to boarding school at sixteen. My co-ed institution was the last of the English boarding schools to offer an on-campus bar for sixth-form students. On Thursdays and Saturdays, hundreds of sixteen to eighteen-year-olds descended on a small basement, claimed their two cans of beer, and rubbed up against each other on a dark, hot dance floor to the music of 'Beenie Man and Other Dance Hall Legends'. My boarding house was conveniently located directly across from the bar, allowing for a quick stagger home at eleven p.m., where our matron would lay out boxes of pizza for us to drunkenly chow together. It also meant that our house garden was utilized as a hedonistic, after-hours playground, and half an hour after curfew, my housemistress would strap a pit helmet on her head and go out into the bushes looking for semi-clothed, fumbling students. After sending any girl caught in the garden to bed with no pizza and returning the lad to his house, there was always a lovely moment when we overheard her contacting the boy's housemaster from her study.

'I discovered your James behind my rhododendron bush with my Emily, his trousers down,' she'd say in her wide Yorkshire accent. 'I have dispatched him on his way; he should be with you in ten minutes.' All of the teachers were aware that we had consumed alcohol before to arriving at the bar. We'd smuggle bottles of vodka in our suitcases disguised as empty, washed-out shampoo bottles, and we had an endless supply of Marlboro Lights beneath our pillows. We disguised the smell of our tracks with cheap perfume and menthol gum; when I smoked a spliff and had bloodshot eyes, I'd wet my hair as if I'd just gotten out of the shower and blame it on the shampoo. The overall unsaid rule was that we trusted you to know your boundaries, so don't be a dick about it. Drink and smoke, but don't act badly or make it evident. Overall, the method worked. There was always the occasional kid who went too far and shattered a chair or attempted to hump a young maths instructor on duty, but the rest of us kept it together. Overall, the lecturers were highly respectful of the students, treating us like young adults rather than children. The last two years of my adolescence were spent at boarding school, and they were the most enjoyable.

University is never going to be the best location for someone with a problematic relationship with alcohol, but my God, I chose the worst one possible when I filed a UCAS application to Exeter. Exeter, located in the verdant, rolling hills of Devon, has long been recognized as a university for half-soaked, semi-literate Hooray Henrys. If you ever encounter a middle-aged man who still plays lacrosse, knows every drinking game rule, and sings better Latin than English when he's drunk, he probably attended Exeter University, also known as 'The Green Welly Uni' in the 1980s. I only applied because Farley did. Farly just applied since it was suitable for Classics and she enjoyed the beach. I only attended because I didn't get into the one course I truly wanted at Bristol, and my parents insisted I go to university.

To this day, I believe that the three years I spent at Exeter made me more foolish than when I arrived. I did little to no work; I went from being an avid reader to not reading a single page of a book that wasn't a set text (and I doubt I even finished one of those). Between September 2006 and July 2009, all I did was drink and shag. All anyone did was drink and shag, taking only brief breaks to eat a kebab, watch an episode of Eggheads, or shop for a fancy-dress outfit for a 'Lashed of the Summer Wine' pub crawl. Far from being the epicenter of radical thought and ardent engagement that I had hoped for, it was the most politically indifferent place I had ever visited. During my entire time there, I was only aware of two protests: the first, a student-body stand against the removal of curly fries from the Student Union Pub's menu, and the second, a young woman's petition to have a bridleway built on campus so she could ride a pony to and from her lectures.

I would bitterly regret the years I wasted at Exeter if it weren't for the one thing that made the entire sad experience worthwhile: the women I met. Within the first week, Farly and I had met a group of females who would become our closest friends. Lacey, a gobby and lovely golden-haired drama student; AJ, a luminous brunette from a rigorous all-girls school who sang hymns when she was drunk; and Sabrina, the charming blonde who was full of life and wide-eyed excitement. Sophie, a red-haired, witty, and boyish South Londoner, was always coming over to mend items in our flats. And then there was Hicks.

Hicks was our ringleader, a Suffolk-born Stig of the Dump with a bleach-blonde bob, crazy eyes in a cape of shimmery blue makeup, long, coltish, teenage legs, and tits I could identify in a line-up because she had them out so often. I'd never encountered anyone like her; she was brazen, dangerous, quick-witted, and audacious. Nothing seemed to have any consequence when you were around Hicks. It was as if she was an empress in her own realm, with her own rules, where the night ended at one p.m. and the next night began the next afternoon, and where an old man you met in a pub became a temporary lodger in your home. She was fully there, incredibly glamorous, and enviably rock 'n' roll. Her impulsive, unlimited desire to have a good time set the tone for the next three years.

The environment at Exeter was so aggressively laddish and macho that I frequently wonder whether that explains why we behaved the way we did as students; whether my all-female circle of friends was attempting to equal that intensity with their behavior. It was a continuation of American frat-boy culture from the films we had grown up watching, intersecting with the obnoxious hierarchical system of public education. We relished group-crouching urination behind skips (Farly and I were once caught and admonished for doing this on the edges of a graveyard, naked bottoms visible to passing cars - regrettably, one of them was a police car). We stole traffic cones that were heaped up in our living room. We snatched one other up and flung each other around the club dance floors. We discussed sex as if it were a team activity. We were full of bravado and rodomontade, and we worked with merciless honesty and zero rivalry toward one another, frequently boring each other's prospective conquests senseless with long, intoxicated lectures about how amazing our friend was.

In the rickety house with the red door where I lived with AJ, Farly, and Lacey, we had a 'visitors' book' for 'overnight guests' to sign when they left the next morning. There was a broken 1980s television in the back garden that sat there, rain or shine. Slugs that blanketed our hallway, which I'd rescue one by one after a night out by taking them outside and placing them in a particular spot of grass (Lacey later acknowledged they put pellets down for them but never told me). It was a period of intense, bizarre debauchery. A world where two of my friends danced all night before going to Exeter Cathedral for a Sunday service and warbling hymns in gold Lycra; a world where Farly once got up at nine a.m. lecture to find me and Hicks still downstairs, drinking Baileys with a middle-aged cab guy we had invited the night before. We were the worst pupils conceivable. We were reckless, self-centered, childish, and fiercely careless. We were Broken Britain, and we used to proclaim it as we marched to the pub. Now, I cross highways and exit tubes early to avoid being in the same vicinity as the boisterous, foolish, self-satisfied exhibitionists that we were.

If I ever wanted to know how widespread the binge-drinking culture was among my university acquaintances, all I had to do was look into the eyes of those who came to visit. My seventeen-year-old brother, Ben, came to stay for a couple of days and was 'appalled' by the half-clothed, barely conscious apparitions he met in the clubs I took him to, particularly an area of one bar nicknamed 'Legend's Corner' because only members of the rugby team were allowed to sit there. He later told my parents that his three-day visit to Exeter was one of the primary reasons he declined to apply to university and instead chose to attend theatrical school.

Lauren traveled to Oxford to study English, and we participated in a university exchange program on several occasions. She'd take the Megabus to Exeter and spend a few days with me, while I'd return to Oxford with her and wander around the Magdalen deer park, fantasizing about an alternate life in which I read books, wrote bi-weekly essays, and lived in a spire-topped house with no television(s). Lauren's first visit was as if I was showing her how to be a student. On a night out, I ordered a bottle of rosé for five quid at the bar.

'OK,' she replied. Is it just for the two of us?'

'No, that's just for me,' I said, as Lauren looked about at my pals, each holding their own bottle of wine and a single plastic glass from the bar. 'We get one each.' The next day, while reclining on the couch eating pricey, sugary, doughy pizza, she watched her first episode of America's Next Top Model. That afternoon, she met the lacrosse player on college who famously started writing his Human Geography dissertation in the pub at 2 p.m. on the day it was due. Lauren claimed she always returned to Oxford feeling comfortable and renewed, having taken a much-needed break from her stressful undergraduate experience of intellectual peacocking. After a few days in Oxford, I always returned to Exeter feeling down and ready to leave.

When describing the bubble of unanswered bad behavior with no penalty that was my undergraduate experience, I frequently refer to a specific episode involving Sophie - now a prominent and recognized writer covering critical LGBTQ and women's issues - to remember how far we've come. One night, after leaving a Thai full moon party at a quayside club dressed as a Thai fisherman, she lay by the water next to a pissed-off male buddy, convinced she was ready to puke due to the eight-shot bucket of Vodka Shark she had just purchased and consumed. To her right was a half-comatose friend of a friend, who was lying on her back like a starfish. Sophie saw an opportunity to both bring a young woman back to safety and possibly get lucky. But as she arrived at the girl's halls of residence, it was evident that this was not going to happen, so she took another cab back to the club and ordered another bucket of Vodka Shark. She then met a boy who said he was going to a nearby late-night curry eatery for takeout. Sophie accompanied him, yelling 'PASANDA, PASANDA' and banged on the shop counter. They ordered their meals, went to his place, and ate a mountain of curry. Sophie vomited into a perspex bowl in the boy's bedroom and left it on the side. She dozed out in his bed, awoke the next morning dressed as a fisherman, peered at the puke bowl but did nothing, then got the boy's micro bike and slid all the way home with glee.

'We were just trying to collect stories for each other,' she says now, when I wonder how we could all have had such an infantile desire for irresponsibility and so little self-awareness. 'That is what we traded in. It wasn't to brag to anyone but each other.'

It was clear that, while everyone enjoyed drinking, I particularly enjoyed drinking. I would consume alcohol at breakneck pace. A lot of it was simply because I like the flavor and sensation of alcohol, but I also drank as a student for the same reason I drank on my own when I was fourteen: putting alcohol into my brain was like pouring water into squash. Everything was diluted and mellowed. The sober girl was filled with anxiety, convinced that everyone she loved would die, and concerned about what others thought of her. The inebriated girl lit a cigarette between her toes 'for a fun' and cartwheeled on the dance floor.

I graduated from Exeter a month before my twenty-first birthday, and by September, I was in London, studying for a Masters in Journalism. This was, believe it or not, the year that my partying peaked; I had been rejected unceremoniously and violently, and I poured myself into weight reduction to distract myself from the grief, and I drank and smoked to do so.

I hadn't lost my taste for it. It was as thrilling at twenty-one as it had been during Natasha Bratt's bat mitzvah eleven years before. I recall sitting on the tube on one of many Saturday nights that year, gazing out at the sparkling metropolis as I traveled from the suburbs to central London on the Metropolitan line, which rode like a cantering horse across the tracks. I believed I owned all of London. Anything's conceivable.

This year's hedonism culminated in an especially un-rock 'n' roll way: a long ride in a minicab. In my defense, Hicks initiated it. In our third year of university, she became a household name among Exeter's student body after leaving a night out at a bar on the High Street, getting into a taxi, and asking the driver to take her to Brighton. She spent every dime she had going there and stayed on the floor of a hotel suite with her married friends who were on a romantic vacation. She returned to Exeter the next week to recount the story.

The night began when my new curly-haired brilliant buddy from my Journalism MA degree, Helen, and I went to our friend Moya's place for a glass of wine and to discuss our revision for an upcoming huge exam. Helen and I proceeded to drink bottle after bottle of wine in the sun, becoming steaming drunk and leaving Moya's at midnight.

I decided the night wasn't finished and I wanted to party, so we boarded a bus from West Hampstead to Oxford Circus. However, as soon as the bus journey began - which also took an unreasonably long time due to a traffic accident - I convinced myself that we weren't on a bus to Oxford Circus, but rather on a coach to Oxford city centre. Helen, rendered similarly to me, agreed with my persuasive theory. Lauren had graduated from Oxford by this point, so I did not call her; instead, I texted a few of her friends whom I had met during my visits there and knew were in their final year. The texts were scarcely understandable, but they went something like this: "My friend Helen and I have accidentally gotten on a coach to Oxford." We're almost there; where is a decent place to go out, and would you like to join us?'

We alighted near the flagship Topshop, which was larger than I remembered from my previous visit to Oxford. We stood outside the shop while I called everyone I had ever met at Oxford University - still not realizing I was in London - but no cigar. Helen and I decided that the night out was a lost cause, but it was too late for me to return the last tube to my parents' house in the suburbs. So we took another bus back to Helen's Finsbury Park flat, which she shares with her partner, and she invited me to sleep on their sofa.

Refusing to let go of my intoxicated fantasy, when I walked into the flat, I assumed we were in Oxford University Halls, and that Helen's friend was still a student here. Helen went to bed, and I checked my phonebook to see if anyone I knew was available for a party. I called my friend Will, a tall, wild, wiry Canadian with long curly hair and eyes as pale as opals. I'd always had a huge crush on him.

'Hello, darling,' he said in his vodka-soaked voice.

'I want a party,' I announced.

'Come here then.'

Where are you?' I asked. 'Aren't you still in university in Birmingham?'

'Warwick. I live in Leamington Spa, he said. 'I will text you the address.'

I walked out of Helen's flat and looked for a taxi service. After 10 minutes of wandering the streets, the alcohol gradually leaving my system as I realized I was in London, not Oxford, I discovered a modest, wooden-fronted minicab firm. I said that I needed a car to take me to Leamington Spa and that money was not an issue - except that it had to be £100 or less because that was all I had in my account and I was at the limit of my overdraft. One of the three befuddled guys stepped behind the glass barrier to retrieve a dusty map of England from his drawer. He unfurled the map and theatrically stretched it across two tables pushed together, much to the amazement of his coworkers. They all clustered around it as one planned the route with dashes in red pen, as if he were the captain of a ship organizing an attack on pirates. Even in my intoxicated state, I thought it was a little over the top.

"£250," he finally announced.

'That's RIDICULOUS,' I replied with pearl-clutching, middle-class customer-rights fury, as if he were the one making the most ridiculous request out of the two of us.

Lady, you want to travel to three counties away at three o'clock in the morning. £250 is an extremely acceptable price.'

I managed to get him down to £200. Will replied he'd pay the remaining £100.

I began sobering up on the M1 at 4 a.m. (There's a statement I hope none of the rest of you have to say or write down in your lifetime). But it was too late to turn back, as I frequently felt in the midst of these small-hour escapades, assuring myself that I was only getting my money's worth out of my youth. A quote by Margaret Atwood hung from the ceiling like a lampshade during this time in my life.

When you're in the middle of a narrative, it's not a story at all, but rather a chaos; a black roaring, blindness, a wreckage of shattered glass and splintered wood; like a house in a tornado, or a boat smashed by icebergs or pushed over the rapids, with everyone on board powerless to stop it. Only later does it resemble a story. When you say it to yourself or others.

It would pay off in the end, I reasoned as I peered out the window on the freeway, the sky turning to dawn. This will provide an endless supply of anecdotes.

I arrived at half past five in the morning. Will met me at the door with five twenty-pound notes. I felt triumphant that I had made it there. The voyage and destination were the focus of the story; what happened afterwards was practically unimportant. We stayed up drinking, talking, and lying in bed half-dressed, smoking pot and listening to Smiths albums, pausing only briefly for some half-arsed snogging. We fell asleep about 11 a.m.

I awoke at 3 p.m. I had a bad headache and a terrible feeling that the punchline to the joke wasn't as humorous as I had thought the night before. I checked my bank account, and it was zero. I checked my phone and saw dozens of worrying texts from pals. I had forgotten I had emailed Farly a photo of me joyously smiling in the back of the cab at four a.m. while flying down the motorway with the message: "QUICK TRIP TO THE WEST MIDLANDS!!'"

I created a plan. My teenage boyfriend, with whom I had maintained a tenuous friendship, was studying medicine at Warwick University. I could remain with him for a few days until some overdue money arrived from my weekend job as a promotion girl, and then catch a train home in time for my Journalism MA exam on Tuesday. But when I texted him, he said he was away on vacation.

My phone rang; it was Sophie.

Is it true you are in Leamington Spa?When I answered the phone, she inquired.

'Yes.'

'Why?'

"Because I wanted an after-party, and my friend Will was having one, and he lives in Leamington Spa." Will, still half sleeping, flashed a closed-eye smile and a guilty-as-charged thumbs up.

'OK, it doesn't make sense,' she replied. 'How are you going to get home?'

I don't know. I was going to stay with an old boyfriend, but he isn't here, and I don't have enough money for the train.' There was a lengthy pause, and I could hear Sophie's concern for me turn to aggravation.

'Okay, I'll book you a bus home then,' she said. Is your phone charged?'

'Yes.'

'I'll provide you the specifics once it's completed.'

'Thank you, thank you,' I replied. 'I will pay you back.'

Sophie booked me a seat on the longest coach ride she could locate, believing that I needed some alone time to reflect on the repercussions of my actions. Much to her displeasure, I landed up on a coach with a rowdy London-bound hen party. During the journey, we all drank tequila shots, and they gave me a sombrero. The next day, when I called Sophie to thank her for rescuing the day, I inquired if she was annoyed by me.

'Dolly,' she continued, 'I'm not furious with you; I'm concerned about you.'

'Why?' I asked.

'Because you were so inebriated, you assumed you were in Oxford city centre when you were actually outside the Oxford Circus Topshop. Do you realize how vulnerable that puts someone? Walking around London that drunk?'

'I'm sorry,' I muttered petulantly. 'I was simply having fun.'

'How many of our friends need to go bankrupt taking cabs around Britain before this madness stops?'

(It would take just one more - Farly, a few months later, from South West London to Exeter. She was in a cab going home from a club when she got a text from a boy she fancied who was still at university, and she asked the driver if he could turn around and go, instead, to Devon. To this day, she shrugs off accusations of extravagance and says the entire journey cost '£90 and a packet of fags'.

But the important thing was that they all told good stories. It was the driving force of my early twenties. I was a six-foot human metal detector looking for fragments of prospective anecdotes, crawling down the earth of existence with my nose pressed against the grass in the hopes of finding something to dig at.

Another night, for £20, Hicks and I went to a swanky London hotel because she had assured it was a hub for 'bored billionaires with buckets of drinks who desire the company of lively, youthful people'. Sure enough, we discovered two middle-aged men from Dubai who ran a curry house on Edgware Road and one of those English language 'universities' over a mobile phone shop on Tottenham Court Road. Hicks and I repeated our old pattern of flamboyantly reciting a well-rehearsed made-up story about how we met on a cruise. I was singing with the band, her husband had thrown himself overboard, and we'd started talking one day while sitting alone on the upper deck, smoking and looking out to sea.

They asked if we wanted to go to their friend Rodney's house, who they assured us was 'a party boy' - a common euphemism for 'generous with his alcohol and drugs'. We all hopped into their waiting car, and the driver drove us to a tower block on Edgware Road, which was far from the Studio 54 promise of excess and grandeur. Hicks and I held hands as we headed to the door, and in the lift, I texted Farly the address of where we were in case something happened to me that night, a morbid ritual she had grown accustomed to.

A Cypriot man in his mid-seventies dressed in stripy pyjamas opened the door.

'My God!" he exclaimed as he checked us over. It's too late!He flung his hands up in despair. 'I am too old for these!'

Our two new acquaintances assured it wouldn't be a long party and that we only wanted a few beers. Rodney generously invited us inside and asked what we wanted to drink. He stated cocktails were his specialty, indicating to his well-stocked 1970s liquor cabinet. I requested a dry Martini.

Rodney captivated me, especially the thousands of framed images of grandchildren sprawled across every possible surface. We wandered about with our Martinis, him still in his pajamas, and he told me the names, ages, and character descriptions of everyone. Meanwhile, Hicks was doing what she always did on nights like this: she was earnestly discussing philosophy with one of the Dubai millionaires, gesticulating dramatically while monologuing about French existentialists, her eyes popping out of her head like forget-me-nots springing from cracks in the sidewalk.

Rodney and I sat on his sofa, and he told me about his past: failed business attempts, the pub he once owned that is now a Waitrose, and the models who shattered his heart. He halted his story at one point, rolled up a five-pound note for the coke he had on his coffee table, and leaned back to gaze at me.

'You know, it's weird; you remind me of a woman I met a few times in the 1970s. She had long blonde hair and eyes that looked exactly like yours. She dated a buddy of mine for a while.

'Oh, yes?I asked, lighting up a cigarette. 'So, who was she?'

'Barby. I believe her name was Barby.' I swallowed, recalling a story my mother had told me about the fun-but-loathsome nickname she was given in her early twenties.

'Barbara,' I responded. 'Barbara Levey.'

'Yes!He yelped. 'Do you know this woman?'

'That's my mum,' I said. I envisioned mom in bed in the suburbs, wondering how she'd react to her daughter getting high with a 75-year-old Cypriot man she met in the 1970s. I went into the other room, interrupted Hicks' one-woman literary salon with her infatuated and apathetic audience, and informed her that we needed to leave right away. She promised a terrific 'after-party' at the curry house one of the men owned on Edgware Road. I told her that we were already at the after-party. I wondered if I had accidently fallen into the dark hinterland of after the after-party and was now trapped there all the time. I was wondering if I needed a ladder out.

But I can't say it was entirely tragic; it wasn't. My companions and I continued to feel that what we were doing was a wonderful act of empowerment and freedom. My mother criticized my attempt to emulate men's snobbish behavior as a form of feminism, stating that it was not a sign of equality. But I still believe there were times when those years of partying were a defiant, joyous, and powerful act; a refusal to utilize my body in the way that was expected of me. A lot of it was just having a great time on our own terms; many of my recollections involve me and one of the females leaving a scenario we were bored with or didn't enjoy in order to spend time together. I was starved for experience, and I satisfied my cravings with like-minded ramblers. And it fostered a gang mentality that none of us have ever shaken.

Some of my recollections are happy, some are painful, and this was the reality. occasionally I danced with a grin on my face till dawn in a circle of my closest friends, and occasionally I fell over on the street while sprinting for the night bus in the rain, lying on the damp pavement for far longer than I should have. Sometimes I knocked myself out going into a lamppost, leaving me with a purple chin for days. But sometimes I awoke in a loving tangle of hung-over girls, full of nothing but comfort and happiness. I occasionally meet folks from those slightly fuzzy years who claim to have spent an evening with me drinking in the corner of a house party, and I immediately panic because I don't remember it. A year or so ago, I shuddered in horror when a black cab driver inquired if my name was 'Donny' since he was very sure he'd picked me up in 'a great state' wandering down a London street with no shoes on in 2009.

But a lot of it was wonderful, carefree entertainment. Much of it was an expedition, through cities, counties, stories, and people, accompanied by a crew of adventurers dressed in neon tights and too much black eyeliner.

And, at the very least, I thought I had demonstrated to everyone that I was an adult. At least I could now be regarded seriously.

THE BAD DATE DIARIES: A HOTEL ON A MAIN ROAD IN EALING

It's my first Christmas after graduating from university, and I work full-time as a sales girl at L.K. Bennett on Bond Street. Debbie, the attractive fashion student who consistently makes the highest commission, paints my lips. Vivien Leigh is in the changing room, getting ready for a major date.

The man's name is Graysen, and I met him at York University a month ago while visiting a school acquaintance. I was waiting at the student union bar to get two vodka Diet Cokes when someone grabbed my hand. Graysen, lanky, pale, and fascinating, with Elvis' eyes smudged in a mist of eyeliner, flipped my palm over.

'There are three youngsters. You'll die at ninety. He stared at me. "You've been here before," he said dramatically.

He is the first person my age I've ever met who chooses not to use Facebook. I believe he is Sartre.

We meet under a large Christmas tree, and he brings me to a Martini bar since he remembers I stated it was my favorite drink (at this point, I'm still in the 'teaching yourself to like Martinis' phase, so I'm worried he'll see my first sip wince, but I manage to hold it together). We then go to the oldest tavern in London, where I drink strawberry beer. He hands me a set of keys; his boss has offered him a hotel room for the night. He never explains why.

Three buses later, in the time it takes him to explain why 'London has been more of a parent to me than my parents have', we arrive at a dismal motel in a converted suburban home on a main road in Ealing. I don't want to sleep with him because I want to get to know him better, so we spend the entire night lying in bed, starring at the off-white ceiling, and discussing our eighteen years together. He is the son of a very elderly, very elegant, very wealthy guy who was 'the last of the colonizers' who discovered a rare sort of fish on his travels, published a book about it, and has lived off the money ever since. I'm agog with astonishment. We fell asleep at five o'clock.

Graysen must leave early the next morning for work. He kisses me goodnight and places a peach pastry on the bedside table. That is the final time we will see one other.

I'll spend the next five years wondering if Graysen was just an actor looking for a credulous audience and an escape from himself for one night. If everything was made up: the palm reading, the hotel, the fish, and the eyeliner.

Then, years later, I'll fall in love with a biology PhD student who will become my lifelong love. One Sunday night, I'll be resting on his bed in his jumper, and he'll pull out a book about a man who discovered a fish to read before we fall asleep. I'll take it from him and check inside to find a photograph of a man with the same face and surname as Graysen. The guy will question why I'm giggling. 'Because it was all real,' I'll explain. 'And that was really ludicrous.'

THE BAD PARTY CHRONICLES: COBHAM, NEW YEAR'S EVE, 2007

'There must be something going on,' I tell Farly as we watch the thirteenth episode of Friends while lying over the sofa at my mother's house at five p.m. on New Year's Eve. 'We're 19 years old; we should be able to find a party anywhere.' I send a supposedly personalized message to everyone in my phone directory. Our friend Dan offers a warehouse rave in Hackney, but Farly is afraid of drug-taking crowds and has never ventured east of Liverpool Street.

Just as we are about to give up hope, someone bites. Felix is a friend from school who was in the year below me and whom I've always had a huge crush on. He mentions a'massive rave in Cobham' and says it's not to be missed. He wants me to bring some female friends. Farly decides to go because it is our only alternative and she knows how much I like Felix. She's taking one for the team and going to the party for the sake of my vagina. We've long employed a mutual, fair, and successful system of turn-taking because we've always been single: I sacrifice my night to enable her pursue a boy, and I bank this act of goodwill so that I may cash it in at any time to have her reciprocate. It undermines democracy. Swings and roundabouts.

We arrive at the enormous detached house in Surrey, the Footballers' Wives belt, to find that it is not a rave, but rather a sedentary oven-pizza party with ten entwined couples and one burly bloke in a rugby shirt playing with the family Labrador.

'Hello!' I say tentatively. 'Is Felix here?'

'He went to the shop to fetch vodka,' the monotonous rugby player says, not glancing up from the dog.

'Weren't you in the year above us at school?' a horsey-faced girl with corkscrew hair inquires.

"Yeah," I answer, cautiously helping myself to a square of pepperoni. 'Are none of your buddies free tonight?'

Felix appears with a clanking carrier bag.

'Hey!' he shouts, reaching out his arms for a hug.

'Hello!' I say, hugging him. This is Farly. Is everyone here in a couple? I murmur through the side of my lips.

'Yeah,' Felix replies. 'We were anticipating a more diverse crowd, but many people who stated they would come haven't shown up.'

'Right.'

'We'll have fun, though!' he adds, wrapping his arms around both of us. 'Three Musketeers.'

The following two hours pass with chummy, intoxicated ease, making me wonder if the lengthy journey to Cobham was worthwhile. Felix, Farly, and I go to the conservatory and play drinking games while we talk and laugh; at one point, he wraps his arms around me, and Farly and I exchange a quick half-smile and flicker of eye contact with her. Enough to have her take a phony phone call upstairs and leave us alone. I could not have loved her more.

'Can I speak with you somewhere quiet?' he says.

'Sure,' I reply, smiling. He grabs my hand in his and leads me out into the garden.

"This is awkward," he adds as I sit on a plastic chair and he leaps from foot to foot.

'Why? Simply say it.'

'I truly fancy your friend Farly,' he says. Is she single? In a moment, I assess how much of a decent person I am.

'No,' I say, deciding that I have plenty of time left in life for personal development. 'No, she is not single.'

'Fuck,' he replies. Is she in a relationship?

'Yes, a very severe one,' I respond sternly while nodding. 'With a boy named Dave.'

"But she was making out in conversation as if she were single?"

'Well, they are no longer officially together,' I say ad lib. But they are still a thing. It's quite intense. She's on the phone with him right now. You know how it can be at New Year's. Consider all of your regrets and unspoken words. Anyway, she's clearly not ready to go on with anyone.

Farly returns to the table, a bottle of wine in hand. A disappointed Felix excuses himself to use the restroom.

'Did you snog him?' she inquires enthusiastically. 'Did I interrupt?'

'No, he fancies you and has asked if you're single, and I've said no because I'm a nasty guy and I don't want you to get off with him, so I've told him you're in a difficult on-off relationship with a boy named Dave, and it's all very sad, and you're not ready to move on with anyone.'

'OK,' she responds.

Is that okay?

'Of course it's fine,' she says. 'He's not my type, anyway.' We hear Felix's footsteps.

'I said you were just on the phone with Dave,' I say in a whisper.

'Yeah,' she says as Felix sits back down. 'So, sure, that was Dave on the phone just now,' she adds robotically, with the nuanced delicacy of a character from Acorn Antiques. 'Again!'

What did he say?

"Oh, same old, same old." Wants me back and believes we can make it work. And I am like, "Dave, we've been here before." Despite the fact that we are not together, I felt something. It just makes it all the more clear to me that I'm not ready to go on with anyone," she says.

Felix fiercely chews his lip before downing the rest of his wine all at once. 'Nearly midnight,' he replies, leaving the table to enter the house. As we recite the countdown, I stand in the heavy, bland, cream suburban living room of this boy I've never met, vowing never to arrange an evening around a prospective conquest again. We watch at the flatscreen television, which is showing BBC coverage of red-cheeked, inebriated people in scarves cheering on the South Bank, and I wish I could be there. Big Ben rings at midnight. The song "Auld Lang Syne" plays. Then, for reasons I'll never understand, everyone in the room begins slow dancing as if it were the last song at the disco. Apart from Felix, who is sitting on the other side of the room, sulking and playing a phone game. I turn the brass handle on the mahogany antique drinks cabinet and take a bottle of whisky. I look across at

Farly, who is holding the family's black Labrador on its hind legs to help it stand up, its paws in her hands. They dance too slowly to the funereal swing of 'Auld Lang Syne'.

We missed the last train back to London, so I stand outside the house and call some local taxi firms for a quote to get home, but they all charge too much. We're stranded in Surrey for at least eight hours in a house full of couples and a crush who doesn't like me, all from the year below me at school. I re-enter the seventh circle of suburbia and observe Farly and the other rugby guy leaning against the fridge before sliding inside the airing cupboard. I go to the garden to smoke the remaining cigarettes on my own.

'Where is Farly?' Felix wonders if anyone else has had the same thought. I can't take the charade anymore.

'She's in the airing cupboard with that rugby player man,' I remark expressionlessly, sipping from the whisky bottle.

'What? What about Dave?

'I dunno,' I reply, igniting my cigarette and expelling smoke into the chilly, motionless night air. 'She and Dave are really complicated, Felix, and the sooner you recognize this the better. It's up, down, on, and off.'

'But she claimed it was on an hour ago,' he responds, outraged.

'Yeah, well, I believe he probably called again, they probably had another fight, and she probably realized she was over it.'

'Great,' he says, settling down on the outdoor chair next to me and smoking a cigarette. 'It's the worst New Year's Eve ever.'

'Yes,' I say. We observe the last of Surrey's fireworks in silence. 'It is.'

BEING A BIT FAT, BEING A BIT THIN

'Do you love me anymore?' I asked.

No, he said. 'No, I do not think I love you anymore.'

'Do you at least like me?' I asked. There was quiet.

I don't think so.

I hung up.

(I've since told people that it's best to lie about this if they're dumping someone; the 'falling out of love' stuff is very horrible, while the 'I don't fancy you' stuff is lethal.)

I was just twenty-one years old and had recently graduated from university. And my first proper boyfriend had just ditched me on the phone.

Harry and I had been dating for a little over a year, despite the fact that we were absolutely and utterly unsuited for each other. He was conservative, fascinated with sports, performed a hundred press-ups before bed every night, was the social secretary of the Exeter University Lacrosse Club, and wore a non-ironic T-shirt with the words 'Lash Gordon' on the front. He despised exaggerated shows of emotion, tall ladies wearing heels, and being overly noisy. So much everything that defined my personality at the moment. He felt I was a disaster, while I believed he was a square.

Our whole relationship was spent arguing, due in large part to the fact that we never spent time apart. He had literally lived in the flat I shared with Lacey, AJ, and Farly during our final year of university, and he had moved into my parents' house for the summer while doing an internship.

One of our lowest points occurred at the conclusion of that long, hot, frantic August with little space between us, when we took a train to Oxford for Lacey's twenty-first birthday celebration. I wandered away from my seat after the main course and came across a swimming pool that looked interesting. So I stripped down and went for a swim, and when a few pals found me, I pushed everyone else to do the same. The night turned into a massive pool party, and I became a sort of naked, poolside Master of Ceremonies. Harry went crazy. The next morning, Farly and AJ huddled behind a tree, uncontrollably laughing as they saw him yell, "YOU WILL NEVER SHOW ME UP LIKE THAT AGAIN!'" at me, my head lowering in humiliation, exacerbated by the fact that the pool had been overchlorinated and my bleached hair had turned a bright bottle green.

We had nothing in common. But he wanted to be my first proper boyfriend, which was a good enough reason for me to date someone at the age of nineteen.

I was living in an East London flat the night he called, staying with a friend indefinitely while starting my journalism course to avoid the lengthy journey from Stanmore. Farly arrived an hour later at one a.m., having driven from her mother's house, and informed me that she was driving me home.

On the way back, I was inconsolable, trying to recall our talk to Farly but remembering almost nothing. My phone rang—it was him. I told her I couldn't communicate with him. She pulled over, scooped it up, and pressed it against her ear.

'Harry, why did you do this?' she exclaimed. I couldn't understand what he was saying on the other end of the call. 'Okay, but why do it to her over the phone? Why couldn't you come see her and do it in person?She barked again. There was more incomprehensible rambling on his end. Farly listened. 'YEAH? WELL, YOU CAN GO FUCK YOURSELF,' she yelled, hanging up and tossing the phone into the seat behind her.

'What did he say?'

'Nothing, really,' she replied.

Farley stayed in my bed that night. And the night after that. She stayed for a fortnight; I did not return to the flat. It was my first experience with heartbreak, and I never imagined the overwhelming feeling of acute bewilderment, as if I had no reason to trust anyone again. I didn't know exactly what had happened or why. I only knew that I hadn't done well enough.

I could also not eat. I'd heard about the consequences of a breakup before, but I had no idea it would affect me. I was and always have been a very hungry girl. Perhaps the most hungry of them. I had never mastered a diet that lasted more than two days. My entire family loved food, as did Farly and I. My mother, a natural cook who grew up with Italian grandparents, began teaching me to cook when I was five years old, standing me next to her on a chair to help knead bread or whisk eggs at the kitchen counter. I cooked for myself in my teens and for everyone at university. When I was six years old, I wrote my first diary entry, which was an enthusiastic account of what I had eaten that day. What was on a plate reminded me of different times in my life: crispy baked potatoes on seaside holidays in Devon, garish, sticky jam tarts on my tenth birthday, and roast chicken on Sunday nights, drowning the dread of the school week in gravy. No matter how bad life became, no matter how excruciating the suffering, I knew I'd always have room for seconds.

I never felt overweight, yet my body type was frequently mislabeled as 'a big girl'. I came from a long line of towering giants. My brother, God love him, was a six-foot-seven youngster who had to shop in stores like 'Magnus' and 'High and Mighty'. By the age of fourteen, I was five foot ten. By the time I was sixteen, I was six feet. But I wasn't one of those adorable tall, lanky teenage part-foal, part-human females; instead, I was broad, with large boobs and hips. I was the complete opposite of the girls featured in Bliss and depicted in The Baby-Sitters Club book series. Just as I was never psychologically equipped to be a teenager, neither was my physical body.

As a teenager, I found it challenging to be so tall since I had no idea how much I was supposed to weigh because every female was half my height and talked about their 'fat weight' as being a weight I hadn't been since childhood, which made me feel ashamed. That, combined with boredom eating and puppy fat, meant I was looking for size 16s when I wasn't quite sixteen. I was aware that I was larger than my friends and had been labeled as overweight, but I always believed that my body would make more sense once I was no longer a child. The only truly mortifying moment came when, at a barbecue aged fifteen, my parents' extremely drunk and spectacularly overweight friend Tilly grabbed my love handles like she was steering the wheel of a ship before announcing to the garden that 'us chunky girls have got to stick together' and telling me in no uncertain terms that 'men like a bit of meat on a girl', before I received a conspiratorial wink from her husband, who was, incidentally, also the width of a Vauxhal

When I went to boarding school, I gradually lost weight, and by the time I came to university, I was a comfortable size 14 - but I didn't mind that I wasn't really slender. I kept kissing the boys I wanted to kiss. I could wear Topshop. And I enjoyed eating and cooking. I realized that was the trade-off.

And yet here I was. Finally, unable to eat anything. From head to toe, I was filled with a sickly yellow sensation, and my appetite, my most valuable possession, had evaporated. My intestines felt agitated. There was a persistent lump in my throat. Mum would offer me bowls of soup in the evening, assuring me it was simple to swallow, but I'd only eat a few spoonfuls and dump the rest down the sink when she wasn't looking.

After a fortnight, I stepped on the scale. I'd lost a stone. I stood naked in front of the glass and saw, for the first time in my life, the very beginnings of what I had been taught were the essential characteristics of femininity. A slimmer waist, hip bones, collarbones, and shoulder blades. In this unfamiliar terrain, where the boy I'd lived a home and life with for over a year was suddenly horrified by me, I had a glimpse of something finally making sense. I had stopped eating, thus my physique was changing. It works. In the midst of the chaos, I discovered a simple formula over which I had complete control. Here was something I could manage that would take me somewhere new, where I could be someone else. The answer was in my reflection: stop eating.

I made a project out of my new purpose; I weighed myself every day, measured my steps and calories, did sit-ups in my bedroom every morning and night, and documented my measurements every week. I lived on Diet Coke and carrot sticks. If I wanted to eat, I would retire to bed or take a hot bath. More weight dropped off. I lost it day by day and pound by pound; it never seemed to stop. This provided me with energy that originally served as a substitute for eating; I felt like a high-speed train running on emptiness. Another month passed, and another stone fell. My period did not arrive, which both worried and encouraged me. At the very least, it meant that something was changing on the inside as well as the outside; I was getting closer to becoming someone new.

When I wasn't at lectures, I hunkered down at home. I still felt delicate after the breakup and didn't want to mingle. Alex, Harry's sister, was the first to detect something was wrong. I had grown close to her over our relationship and, happily, she stood by me through our breakup. She had just moved to New York, and we were skyping every day. One day, in the middle of one of our conversations, I stood up, revealing my entire body for the first time in months.

Where are your tits?' she inquired, her eyes widening as she inspected me up and down while leaning into her camera.

'They are there.'

'No, they are not. And your stomach resembles an ironing board. Dolls, what has happened?'

'Nothing; I merely lost some weight.'

'Oh, sweetie,' she replied, frowning. 'You're not eating, are you?'

Others were less perceptive. I began to go out more and see people from university. People informed me they had heard about Harry and were sorry. People informed me that he had a new girlfriend. People repeatedly complimented me on my appearance. Every compliment fueled me like a meal.

I went out and drank constantly in an attempt to distract myself from the ache of hunger. My mother became increasingly concerned and would leave plates of food on the kitchen table for me when I returned home from a night out. She correctly assumed that I would be more likely to eat then. I learned to go directly to bed when I arrived home. By December, I had lost three stones. Three stones in three months. I found it difficult to summon the ideas and tight routines that had kept me away from food up to that point. I was fatigued, my hair was thin, and I was always bone-chillingly cold. I sat in the shower to warm myself up, but the water was so hot that it burned my back and left marks. I routinely lied to my frightened parents about how much I'd eaten that day and when I was going to eat again. I would dream that I had ingested mountains and mountains of food, only to awaken in tears of anguish because I had mistakenly shattered the spell I had established.

Hicks remained at Exeter for an additional year after the rest of us graduated. Sophie, Farly, and I decided to drive down and spend the weekend with her, visiting all of our old haunts. It also meant I could see Harry, who was in his final year, which I hoped would feel like a full circle and provide me with some closure. When I told him we needed to return our belongings to each other, he agreed to meet with me.

The girls took me to his place early on Saturday evening and parked outside.

'WE'LL WAIT RIGHT HERE, MATE,' Hicks said out the car window, her feet and a cigarette dangling from it. I went to Harry's front door and rang the doorbell.

'Oh my God,' he murmured as he opened the door. 'You look—'

'Hello, Harry,' I said, walking past him and up the stairs. He followed behind me. We stood at opposite sides of his bedroom, starring at one another.

'You look wonderful.'

I replied, 'Thank you. 'Can I get my things?'

'Yeah, yeah, sure,' he replied in a stupor. He handed me a small bag containing my clothing and books. I removed his rolled-up jumpers from my handbag and placed them on his bed.

'That's all your stuff I found in my house.'

'Okay, thanks,' he replied. 'How long are you here?'

It's the weekend. Me, Farly, and Sophie are staying with Hicks.

'Oh, terrific,' he replied. He was speaking in an uncharacteristically modest tone. 'Well, please send them my love. Although, they probably don't want to hear from me." There was a lengthy stillness as we stared at each other. 'I'm sorry for—'

'Don't be," I snapped.

'I am,' he answered. 'I apologize for the way I handled it.'

'Honestly, don't be, you did me the greatest favor,' I exclaimed. 'Look, I've even grown my nails, I don't bite them anymore, and I got my first manicure, would you believe it, for only five pounds,' I said, aggressively pushing my hands out towards him. I heard a car honk outside. Sophie and Hicks were sipping tinnies and blaring the horn, while Farly flew around, attempting to stop them.

'I have to go,' I said.

'Certainly,' he responded. We proceeded silently down the steps, and he unlocked his front door.

'Are you okay?' he asked. 'You look really—'

'Thin?' I asked.

'Yeah.'

'I'm good, Harry,' I replied before giving him a quick hug. 'Goodbye.'

The girls took me out for a curry to commemorate what they viewed as the grand conclusion of the entire miserable disaster; I nibbled at rice and drank pint after pint of beer. I felt more upset, ashamed, angry, and out of control than before. Whatever I was hoping to achieve by visiting him had not worked. I hadn't received it.

I threw myself into losing weight harder and faster. My rage fuelled me. My weight began to plateau, indicating that the cogs of my metabolism were confused and slowing down, so I ate even less. Friends started confronting me about it, and Farly told me she believed I was obsessed. She tried to encourage me to open up, but I dismissed her questions with laughter. In general, I discovered that making jokes about how little I ate was a fantastic way to get people off my back. I would bring it up before anyone else did, so they understood it wasn't an issue, but rather a diet. And, as I repeatedly pointed out, I was still a size 10. I wasn't underweight; I simply started out huge.

I persevered because it was the only thing I could control. I carried on because I just wanted to be happy, and everyone knows that being slimmer makes you happier. I persisted because society was praising me for the misery I had inflicted on myself. I received praises and propositions, felt more accepted by strangers, and almost all clothes looked amazing on me. I felt as if I had finally earned the right to be regarded seriously as a woman, and that everything before that had been unnecessary. That I had been naive to believe I was ever deserving of affection. I had linked love with thinness, and to my horror, evidence of this notion was everywhere. My health was deteriorating, but my investments were rising.

The difficulty is that a woman can never be truly slim. It is not considered a significant price to pay to be constantly hungry, to restrict an entire food group, or to spend four nights a week at a Fitness First gym. To be an empirically handsome young man, all you need is a nice grin, an average body type (give or take a stone), some hair, and a decent jumper. To be a desirable woman, the sky is the limit. Have every part of your body waxed. Have a manicure every week. Wear heels every day. Even if you work in an office, you can still look like a Victoria's Secret Angel. It isn't enough to be an average-sized woman with some hair and a decent jumper. That doesn't cut it. We're told we have to look like the women who are paid to look that way in their profession.

And the more flawless I tried to be, the more flaws I discovered. I had more body confidence as a size 14 than when I was three stone lighter. When I went naked with a new partner, I wanted to apologize for what I had to offer and list a series of things I'd alter, like a middle-class hostess who says, 'Oh, don't look at the carpet, the carpet's absolutely horrible, I promise it's all going to improve,' when she has friends over. Some of my friends' concerns began to blend with irritability. I arrived at gatherings half-dressed, having not eaten anything in days, and would walk about in a trance, barely able to speak. Sabrina and AJ went traveling together, and I arrived late to their farewell party, felt too faint to speak with anyone, created an excuse, and departed after half an hour. I could feel myself pushing away from my life and becoming increasingly absorbed in a completely false sense of control. And then I fell in love for the very first time.

When I first met Leo, I was strolling around a grungy house party in Elephant & Castle. I'd never seen a man more perfect. Tall and lean, with dark floppy hair, a strong jaw, dazzling eyes, a retroussé nose, and a seventies tache; a face that was half Josh Brolin and half James Taylor, with - and here's the best bit - no awareness of his own beauty. He was a hippie PhD candidate, a monomaniac with a monobrow.

We started seeing each other shortly after that night. I knew it was serious since I hadn't gone to bed with him in two months, wanting badly to get it perfect, to appreciate every bit of our time together rather than rush through anything. He lived in Camden, and after one of our nights together, usually around four a.m., he'd accompany me to the bus stop outside Chalk Farm station, where I'd wait for the N5 to take me ten miles north to Edgware. From there, I'd walk 45 minutes west to Stanmore, meandering through the quiet streets lined with Volkswagens and watching the sun rise over the semi-detached red-brick houses, and I was happier than I could have dreamed.

One night, as we were walking around Camden, he stopped to kiss me and ran his hands through my hair, feeling the bumps from my clip-in hair extensions. He took the heavy hair from my face and tucked it behind my head.

'You'd look great with short hair,' he commented.

'No way,' I responded. 'When I was a teenager, I had a bob and resembled a monk.

'No, I'm talking really briefly. You should do it.

'Nah,' I replied. 'I do not have the face for it.'

'YOU DO!' he replied. Don't be a scaredy cat. It's only hair.

He had no idea that 'simply hair' was all I considered myself capable of. Just hair, collarbones, and sit-ups. 'Just' was all I'd spent my energy on for the better part of a year, and it was all I thought I deserved.

A month later, I brought a photo of Twiggy to the hairdresser, drank a shot of vodka, and had my hair cut fifteen inches shorter. With it went some of my fixation with my appearance. It cut off and fell on the ground.

Leo had not grasped my secret since I didn't want him to think I was crazy, but after a few months of dating, he added a few details. I managed to avoid any situations involving food; whenever we parted ways in the morning, I always told him I'd eat breakfast later. Finally, a friend informed him that she suspected I was ill.

Is this a problem?He questioned me.

'It's okay,' I murmured, ashamed and terrified that I was about to lose the best person I'd ever met.

'Because I can accomplish this with you. I can help you. But I can't fall in love with you if you're not talking to me.

'OK, there's been an issue,' I told him. 'But things will change. 'I promise.

I would have given anything to keep this man in my life. The love I felt was forceful and tense; I loved him with panic and desire. I did not fall in love; rather, love fell on me. Like a ton of bricks from a considerable height. I had no alternative but to let go of a passion that was about to destroy everything.

So, I did. I read the necessary books and went to the doctor. A stone slowly crept back on me. I gradually got acclimated to eating properly. My health has restored. I even tried group support meetings in community centers, where, believe it or not, the first thing they do is place a plate of biscuits in the middle of the room and argue about whose turn it is on the rota to bring the snacks the next week, which seemed to me to be as useful as putting a bottle of Jack Daniel's in the middle of an AA meeting.

I fell back in love with cooking. I fell back in love with eating. Every weekend, I would do both with Leo. My mother and I watched old Fanny Cradock and Nigella programs together. Everyone kept telling me I looked 'healthy' whenever they saw me, and I tried to ignore the fact that this meant I was obese again. The war was over, and the recuperation began. I got my life back.

My hippy experience freed me from my addiction to perfection. We'd get drunk and chop my hair further shorter. He'd chop large chunks out with kitchen scissors while I sat at the table, squeezing limes into beers. I eventually shaved both sides, resulting in a tufty mohawk. I lived in plimsolls and his sweatshirts, and I spent days with him without touching a make-up bag or a razor, which was a first. We'd spend weekends at the coast, washing our faces, bodies, and dishes in the water. We set up a tent in his bedroom on Sunday nights since we were bored. It was pure, unfettered, and perfect.

But I knew deep down that I was still transforming at the command of a man's gaze; I had simply moved to the other extreme of the spectrum. Leo despised me for wearing too much make-up, so I'd wipe it off on the bus home after a party. I'd change out of my heels for high-tops.

I didn't want to regain the weight I had lost. If I hadn't met Leo, I believe I would have continued to lose weight, but he helped me recover completely. As I grew older and became more conscious of how valuable a strong functional body is, I felt humiliated and perplexed that I could have mistreated mine so horribly. But it would be a lie to claim that I believe I will ever be completely free of what occurred at that time, which no one ever tells you. You can improve your physical health by developing a sensible, balanced, and caring attitude toward weight as well as excellent daily practices. However, you must remember how many calories are in a boiled egg and how many steps are required to burn how many calories. You can't forget how much you weighed every week of the month. You can try as hard as you can to block everything out, but on really terrible days, it feels like you'll never be as joyful as the ten-year-old sucking colorful jam from her fingertips again.

EVERYTHING I KNEW ABOUT LOVE AT TWENTY-ONE

Men admire a wild, filthy lady. Have sex on the first date, stay up all night, smoke hash in their bed in the morning, never call them again, tell them you hate them, show up on their doorstep dressed like an Ann Summers nurse, and be everything but conventional. This is how you keep people interested.

If you ignore your best friends' boyfriends for long enough, they will ultimately leave. Treat them as you would a normal cold or a moderate case of thrush.

A breakup will never be as difficult as the first one. In the months that follow, you'll drift around aimlessly, feeling as lost and confused as a child, questioning everything you thought you knew and thinking about all you need to relearn.

Always stay at a man's residence, and leave whenever you want in the morning.

The ideal man is olive-skinned, with brown or green eyes, a large, powerful nose, a thick beard, and curling dark hair. He has no humiliating tattoos and five pairs of vintage Levi's.

When you are not having sex, have a bush that resembles a wild, climbing shrub. It's pointless to waste time, money, and fumes on hair removal lotion unless the effects are visible.

When you are skinny enough, you will be satisfied with yourself and hence worthy of love.

Don't go out with someone who won't allow you to drink and flirt with other people. If that is part of your identity, people should accept you as you are.

Orgasms are simple to fake and make both parties feel better. Do something good today.

When you fall in love with the right man, you will feel at ease, balanced, and tranquil.

Being dumped is the absolute worst feeling in the world.

Men, on the whole, cannot be trusted.

The initial three months of a relationship are the most enjoyable.

A good friend would always prioritize you over a man.

When you can't sleep, imagine all the love encounters you'll have with olive-skinned, curly-haired males in the future.

GOOSEBERRY FOOL: MY LIFE AS A THIRD WHEEL

It started with a train ride. I always imagined that something wonderful would happen to me on a train. The transitional state of a lengthy journey has always struck me as the most beautiful and mystical of places to be; marooned in a cosy pod of your own thoughts, suspended in mid-air, passing through a jumble of silent, blank pages between two chapters. A place where phones fade in and out of consciousness and you are forced to spend time with your ideas, determining what has to be reshaped and reorganized. I have had tremendous dreams when sitting on trains. The clearest moments of insight or thankfulness have come to me when driving across unknown English countryside, peering out over a golden rapeseed field, contemplating what I am leaving behind or about to approach.

In 2008, I boarded a train at Paddington that changed my life forever, but not in the way I expected. It was not at all like Before Sunrise, Some Like It Hot, or Murder on the Orient Express. I didn't fall in love, perform a raunchy, boozy rendition of 'Runnin' Wild' on the ukulele, or become entangled in a murder mystery; instead, I set off a chain of events that would unfold slowly over the next five years, until the story was so frustratingly far away that I couldn't touch it, let alone undo what I had started. The narrative of the train voyage that altered my life isn't really about me.

It was the coldest winter I had ever experienced (possibly due to my preference for form-fitting bodycon dresses at the time), and it began to snow as I was on the last Sunday-night train from London to Exeter University. The train broke down just outside Bristol, and while other passengers groaned, huffed, and stomped around in irritation, I couldn't have imagined a more lovely scene. I purchased a bottle of cheap red wine from the First Great Western buffet carriage and returned to my seat to gaze out at the inky, silent countryside, which was neatly covered with thick snow like icing on a Christmas cake.

On the seat across from me, there was a boy my age with the most beautiful face I'd ever seen. He had been trying to catch my eyes as I had been staring out the window, dreaming about a man on this broken-down train attempting to catch my gaze. Finally, he grabbed my attention, introduced himself as Hector, and offered to join me for a drink.

He exuded a unique, unwavering confidence that had clearly been acquired at a public school. It's the assurance that comes from being handed an old jacket of identity at the age of thirteen, complete with house colors, a crass moniker, and a motto that can be remembered in song even after five pints. It's the brazen confidence that comes from being in a debating society at the age of thirteen, which eventually elbows its way to the top of government; the sort that convinces you it has a right to be here and has something to say. Fortunately, Hector's arrogance might be countered by his cherub features: dazzling blue eyes with cornflower irises and an upturned nose reminiscent of a boy in a 1950s soap commercial. He had the curling, floppy hair of a young Hugh Grant and a rich, plummy, humorous voice. We talked for two hours on the train, laughing, drinking, and eating the mince pies my mother had prepared for me.

I get what you're thinking: if only this encounter had been more twee. That was also on my mind when I was nineteen years old. So, inspired by the numerous romcoms shown on terrestrial television on Sunday nights, I believed it would be a serendipitous gesture if we didn't share numbers and hoped to be reunited by coincidence. And off he went, into the chilly night at Bristol station, leaving me with enough fodder to write about in my rambling, anonymous'single girl's travels' blog for at least three articles.

Two years to the month, a few months after Harry and I split up, I was standing at the bar of a pub on Portobello Road when he strolled in. Even after only two years, his cherubic face had turned sardonic and attractive when matched with a more mature suit and coat, as well as a slightly less floppy haircut.

'Of all the pubs in the world,' he remarked, approaching me and kissing both cheeks. As history would have it, we spent the night sipping cheap red wine while the snow fell steadily outside, and then we were stranded once more. The snow made it impossible for me to catch a bus home, and I was too inebriated to play hard to get. He tossed me over his shoulder like a Persian shawl and we returned to his flat, unable to face the snow in his unstable, cheap heels.

By four a.m., we were still up, laying naked on his floor, chain smoking American Spirits and flicking ash into a cup placed on my stomach. He pulled my eyeliner from my bag and drew a line from Ted Hughes' poetry on his wall. The words hung, slurred and smeared in kohl, alongside multiple charcoal drawings of a naked woman. ('I did them. They're my ex,' he boasted, as I lay naked as his current project, staring up at his wall of artefacts of shags gone by. 'Sweet girl, shame she was married.') Next to his bed there was a black leather address book with three words embossed in gold on the front: BLONDES, BRUNETTES, REDHEADS. You had to hand it to him - he may have been a shagger, but he was an imaginative shagger.

Hector was waggish, impish, boyish, caddish, rakish, and roguish— all adjectives you'd use to characterize a man in a Noel Coward comedy. I'd never met someone like him before. Everything about him was antiquated: his family held titles, he wore a floor-length wolf fur coat from Russia that belonged to his grandfather, and his shirts bore boarding school logos. Everything in his room was used or borrowed. Even his profession was borrowed; his employer was the ex-toy-boy boyfriend of his ex-socialite mother, who had given this catastrophic graduate a job in the City out of love for her. I used to leave Hector in the morning and wonder what he was doing at work in between flouncing around in my underwear, which he wore beneath his (unpressed) trousers, and sending me dirty emails all day from his work account.

Our relationship was wholly nocturnal because he was completely nocturnal, like a fabled beast of the night or a wandering wolf skinned for his coat. We went out and drank at dark pubs, and our dates started at midnight. I once showed up at his place naked, under a trench coat. I was twenty-one and living out a Jackie Collins story, playing alongside an overgrown, randy Just William.

He never met my friends, and I never met his, which suited us perfectly. I had no idea he had housemates until I fell drunkenly into the kitchen one morning at six a.m., completely nude, and was greeted by a man named Scott. I slammed the door and turned on the light to see him seated in his suit, eating cereal and reading the paper before work. Hector found it amusing; more than that, he found the prospect of his housemate seeing me naked in front of him appealing. We had our first row.

A few days later, I was preparing scrambled eggs in his kitchen when Scott arrived in his dressing robe. He gave me an apologetic smile.

'Hello,' he said with an uneasy wave.

'Hello,' I responded. 'I am very sorry about the other morning. Hector informed me that no one was in. I was really upset with him.

It's fine. Honestly, it's fine.

'It's not fine, it's terrible, and I'm very sorry,' I said. 'This is the last thing you want to see before work.'

"It was a pleasant surprise," he stated. I offered him eggs and toast as an olive branch.

We sat and made polite chat, which led us to the topic of dating. Was he seeing anybody? No. Did I have any nice single pals that he could date? Yes, I did have the perfect gal. My best pal, Farly.

'But she's not seeking for a relationship right now; she's ok being single, so it would be a more casual affair,' I warned.

'That sounds great.'

'Great! I'll give you her number. It's the least I could do,' I explained. I entered her number into his phone. Why not? He appeared like a good guy: beautiful and respectful. She presumably wanted a fling. I stated it briefly to her and then forgot about it.

I believe it is crucial that I halt here to explain why I am single-white-female for the remainder of this story.

My bond with Farly did not happen overnight; she spent her first year of school tightly connected to a gang of Power Princesses. They were a type of North London suburban girl that dominated school. They wore blonde highlights, Tiffany jewelry, and told stories about Brady, a social and sports club in Edgware for Jewish teens known as the Chinawhite of the suburbs. I, on the other hand, wore a lot of black on weekends and spent time at school inventing performances in the theater department, attempting to represent the trauma of a plane crash with only a wood block. However, we were assigned to the same French and arithmetic classes, and we quickly learned that we shared a sense of humour as well as a love of The Sound of Music and watermelon lip balm.

Our off-hours acquaintance began gingerly after a few months of sitting next to one other in class. I invited her over to my house first, and my mother prepared roast chicken. My father did what he does with all of my friends: he clutches onto one detail about them in a frenzy to discover a common language and brings it up in every other phrase. With Farly, this is everything related to Jews or Judaism, which he has done for around ten years, stating things like, "Have you seen Sir Alan Sugar's decision to downsize Amstrad?" Great shame," or "I recently saw an advertisement for reduced airfares to Tel Aviv." Must be great, hot weather there right now.' But after a slow start, we were inseparable. We spent every time we could together at school, and when we came home, we wolfed down our dinners before calling each other to discuss whatever else we had forgotten to address during our several meetings during the day. This process was so engrained that I can still recall Farly's mother's landline number from 2000 to 2006 faster than I can remember my credit card pin.

I despised school and was frequently in trouble. After a suspension, a fight with my deputy principal, and a detention at the age of twelve, I returned to geography studies with a teacher who detested me. We were requested to take out our exercise books, which I had forgotten to pack, as I did with everything as a child. I was a disaster. Every year at the Christmas party, a bin bag was presented as 'The Dolly Alderton Prize for Disorganization'. The chosen student had to travel throughout the school and collect all of her possessions that she had left laying around. I despised it.

Where is your exercise book?' the teacher inquired, staring down at my desk, her unpleasant breath tinged with Nescafé and smokes.

'I forgot it,' I mumbled.

'Oh, there's a surprise,' she exclaimed, raising her voice to the level of a public announcement and striding around the classroom. 'She had forgotten it. Has there ever been a day in your life when you didn't forget something? It's only one book, and it's not tough.' She slapped her board rubber down on her desk.

My face flushed, and I felt the growing discomfort of holding hot tears in the back of my throat. Farly squeezed my palm beneath the table twice, quickly and firmly. I understood what it meant. A worldwide, silent Morse code for "I'm here, I love you." At that point, I understood everything had changed: we had transitioned. We'd chosen each other. We were family.

Farly and I had always been each other's plus ones, every day of our lives. We were each other's sidekicks at every family gathering, holiday, and party. We've never rowed properly unless we were drunk on a night out. We've never lied to each other. In almost fifteen years, I've never gone more than a few hours without thinking about her. I only make sense with her present to serve as my counterpoint, and vice versa. Without Farly's affection, I am nothing but a jumble of torn and half-finished thoughts; of blood, muscle, skin, and bone, unattainable goals, and a stack of garbage teenage poetry under my bed. My disarray only gets proper shape when that familiar and cherished element of my life stands beside me.

We know the names of all our grandparents and childhood toys, as well as the exact phrases that, when spoken in a specific order, cause us to laugh, cry, or shout. She has not left a single rock on the shore of my history untouched. She knows where to find everything in me, and I know where all of her belongings are too. She is, simply put, my best buddy.

Valentine's Day 2010. Scott and Farly chose that day for their first date. I mean, who does that? I'm not sure why they went on a date; I thought the drink was just a formality; all they were doing was meeting up for a one-night stand.

'I realize it sounds crazy,' she said. 'But we've been texting back and forth for a while, and this is the only day we can both do.'

Where are you going?'

I don't know. He's going to pick me up from work and recommended a lovely restaurant in Notting Hill for supper.

'DINNER?' I yelled. Why are you going out for bloody DINNER? I assumed this was just going to be a shag?'

'Well, Doll, I can't just go around to his place; I need to talk to him first.'

'But why dinner? It's not like we're forty. Such a waste of money. Also, why Valentine's Day?'

'I told you, else we'd have to wait for decades; we're both really busy.'

'"We're both very busy,"' I mimicked. 'You act like you're married.'

'Oh, shut it.'

'Don't you think it'll be strange if he - a man you've never met - meets you at work and takes you out to dinner on VALENTINE'S DAY among a slew of other couples? Don't you think it will affect your perception of whether or not you like him?'

'No. It is going to be really informal.

The dinner went great. The supper was not at all casual. Scott picked

Farly up at Harrods, where she was working on a jewellery counter in the rain. They took a cab to Notting Hill, went to the restaurant, and enjoyed the nicest date Farly had ever had. I knew that was the best date Farly had ever had because she didn't go on and on about it. When I inquired about Scott, she was hesitant. Measured. She even sounded like an adult.

The aggravating adultness of Farly and Scott's courtship made me realize how ridiculous my relationship with Hector had become. Hector's 'ishes' went off like milk: selfish, oafish, and frightening. He was too terrible, and the act was no longer entertaining; I didn't want to drink a bottle of white wine for breakfast, smack him over the head with a loafer in a play fight, or pretend to be a naughty pixie as part of his wacky, overcomplicated sexual fantasies. Twice in a week, he got drunk, passed out, and locked me out of his house in the rain for the better part of the night. The ideal head-boy assurance came with an additional requirement: a matron. That was not the job for me.

'Please, Dolly,' Farly pleaded on a Friday night out. 'Please see him for one more night.'

'No,' I replied forcefully. 'I don't fancy him anymore.'

'Oh, but Scott and I aren't at the point where I can just walk around to his flat; I'd appear like a stalker.'

'It's never disturbed you before.' (Farly once handed a man £20 in phone credit and made him promise to text her, which he never did.)

'Yes, but I want to be normal with him,' she explained genuinely. 'I'm acting normal with him, which is really good. Please text Hector. We could go round together; it wouldn't be weird.' I considered it. 'Come on, I already did this for you.'

Damn her to hell, she did.

I texted Hector to say I was bringing Farly. We boarded a night bus to Notting Hill.

Predictably, after the four of us had a drink together in their living room, with Hector rambling on about the history of nipple clamps in his obnoxious, drunk Nigel Havers accent and Farly doing her best hair-twirling and bashful smile at Scott, the two of them headed off. Hector escorted me to his bedroom, saying he wanted to 'show me something'. He was acting unusually emotional and needy, as men like him do when they notice you've become distant (I hadn't answered his obscene limerick emails in over two weeks). I sat on his bed, drinking warm white wine directly from the bottle.

'What is this?' I asked simply. He picked up a guitar. Oh no. Not this; anything but this. The bedroom I had spent months fantasizing about and wishing I could be in had suddenly transformed into a cave of my own particular nightmares. I quickly recognized the bohemian mess for what it was: soiled socks scattered over the floor, a faint odor of mould that smelled like an old cricket pavilion on a damp day, and a comforter with holes burned from unconscious chain smoking. The lovely charcoal drawings of naked women had transformed into nasty, knowing gargoyles gazing down at me. We had to go through it, and now you do too, they hissed.

'There's something I want you to hear,' he mumbled and struck two furious notes while attempting to tune his guitar.

'Oh God, it's fine, you don't have to.

'Dolly Alderton,' he said, as if he were at an open mic night. 'I'm very smitten. I wrote this song for you." He began playing the three-chord pattern he had previously played me repeatedly.

'I saw her on a train,' he sung with an Americana croak. Life would never be the same. After the first night, we --

'Hector,' I replied sullenly, feeling the liquor hit me full force. "I think we should stop seeing each other."

I went with Farly early the next morning, and I never saw him again. Farly and Scott informed me that I had truly broken his heart, and an overnight guest's Mulberry Bayswater purse did not appear on the kitchen table for at least three weeks.

(Footnote: Hector is now a highly wealthy entrepreneur and married to a Hollywood star, which I discovered while sitting in my jammies eating a whole chocolate yule log by myself: go figure.)

THINGS I AM SCARED OF

- Dying - People I enjoy dying, but I feel guilty about saying negative things about people who have passed away. Drunk men on the street have told me I'm tall, fat, sexy, ugly, to cheer up, want to shag me, or would never shag me. - Drunk individuals 'putting on' (taking) my hat at parties. - Losing jewelry: Falling from a window - Accidentally murdering a baby – Parlor games - Discussing the history of American politics -- Starting fires everywhere. Not understanding the washing machine. Cancer

Possible risks include STDs, chewing on wooden lollipops, plane crashes, and plane meals.

- Working in an office - Being asked about my beliefs in God, horoscopes, and why I believe them. Going into an unplanned overdraft - Never having a puppy.

BEING BJÖRN AGAIN

After I stopped seeing Hector, I figured it was just a matter of time before Farly and Scott fell apart. I had been the glue that held them together, and when I left that dirty block of flats in Notting Hill, I believed they had little in common. However, within a few weeks, Farly casually mentioned that they were planning a mini-break to Cambridge. Jealousy flooded my bloodstream, making my entire body sting like vinegar. I had always had a boy on the scene, but she now had a legitimate, older boyfriend. No one wore her knickers to work, forced her to wear a fishnet body stocking, didn't know her surname, or texted her once a week. Farly had a guy that spent more time with her sober than not sober, took her on mini-breaks, called her instead of texting, and wanted to have real talks with her.

'What's even in Cambridge?' I complained bitterly to AJ. What about a Bella Italia? Well, good luck. Have fun.

'What is he like?' AJ inquired. To be honest, I knew very little.

'Bad news,' I stated sadly. 'Too old and serious for her.'

And then, three months later, practically to the day, he confessed his love for her. She announced it at a dinner with friends. We all toasted it and yelled with joy; on the night bus home, I penned a sorrowful soliloquy about it in my iPhone notes.

Although I had despised watching Farly be mistreated by ignorant teenage lads throughout the years - being led on, ignored, and dumped - I understood there was some safety in it. As long as boys didn't take her seriously, I could have her all to myself. I was completely fucked the moment an adult man with a brain stopped and expressed an interest in her. How could he not be in love with her? She was lovely and witty. She was the nicest person I knew; she had spent years loan me money to get me out of trouble and picking me up in her car at three a.m. when my bus home had stopped. She had the qualities of the ideal partner: she put people first, listened, and remembered things. She wrote notes in my packed lunch box before I left for work and sent cards to express how proud she was of me.

I had always made boys like me by using smoke and mirrors, exaggeration and bravado, heavy make-up, and excessive drinking. There was no pretense or deception with Farly; if a male fell in love with her, he did so from the first date, whether he realized it or not. She was my best kept secret, and now it was revealed.

We had our first row since adolescence at a Christmas gathering at our friend Diana's place the next year. I was there with Leo. She arrived late with Scott, and this was the first time I'd seen her in a month. I made no outward effort to greet her, instead watching them from the corner of my eye. I made it a point to laugh loudly at very unfunny things so she knew I was there and having a lot of fun without her.

When she came over, the discussion was stilted and abrupt.

'Why are you avoiding me tonight?' she finally said.

'Why are you neglecting me for a year?' I responded.

'What are you talking about?' I texted you yesterday.

'Oh yeah, texting. You are exceptional at texting. Texting is your "get out of jail free" card, which means you don't have to see me for months and go to Scott's flat every night, and when someone questions you about it, you can say, "Oh, but I text her." "I text her every day.

"Can we do this upstairs?" she snarled.

I refilled my plastic cup with Glen's vodka and a dash of Coke before stomping up to Diana's room. For two hours, we shouted at each other. We started out loud, then went quieter, till we were too enraged and tired to go on, so we made up. I told her she had abandoned me, and I used a convoluted metaphor to explain how I had learned she had always thought of me as Björn Again.

'What does that even mean?' she exclaimed.

'Björn Again. They were the warm-up band for the Spice Girls concert we both attended. They were horrible, and we couldn't wait for it to end. I've realized I've only been your warm-up act for eleven years, until your headliner arrived. "You've never been my warm-up act; you've always been my Spice Girls, and I wish I'd known sooner so I could have put you down the bill and MADE YOU BJÖRN AGAIN."

She told me I was being emotional, and that she was allowed to have her first relationship. I told her she could have her first boyfriend; I just hadn't expected her to prioritize him over everyone else. We emerged with our faces plastered like Jackson Pollock had sprayed a gallon of mascara on canvases. Scott and Leo stood silently at the bottom of the stairs, clearly exhausted from football and light conversation about current events. We grabbed them and our coats, then departed separately. Years later, Diana informed me that they had turned down the music downstairs so that the entire party could hear the debate.

'He's her boyfriend,' my infuriatingly reasonable academic boyfriend said as we took the long walk back to his Stockwell flat while sipping tinnies. 'They are in love, and she has transformed. That's okay; it's part of growing up.

'You're my boyfriend,' I snapped. I'm in love. I have not changed. She remains the most significant person in my life. I still want to see her the most. I do not prioritize my relationship.

He drank from his can of beer.

'Maybe that's not typical,' he said.

Leo and I ended our relationship after two years together. I had tried everything I could to make it work, but so much had changed since we first met as undergraduates at a house party in Elephant & Castle. We had both grown up and become very different people.

For nine months after finishing journalism school, I worked as an unpaid chair-filler for several magazines and newspapers under the pretense of job experience. I had been turned down as an intern at Tatler, an editorial assistant at Weight Watchers magazine, and a waiter at a nearby Pizza Express. To sustain myself, I returned to my former job as a promo girl, strolling down former Brompton Road with a group of unemployed West End dancers and air hostesses, handing out brochures for a rib restaurant. I quit the day they forced me to dress up as a pig and was attacked by anti-fur activists outside Harrods.

I was desperate for a job. It was all I thought about from the moment I awoke till I fell asleep in my childhood bedroom. I wanted for a career in my early twenties with the same fervor as I did for my first boyfriend in my early teens, obsessing over who I knew who had one and grilling them on how they got it. Lying in bed night after night, thinking how many more years this may last.

Finally, one early evening, I was standing on a train platform and received a call from an unknown number. It was Tim, a story producer for E4's new structured reality series Made in Chelsea. I had written a series of online evaluations of the first season (again, paid in the post-grad currency of 'exposure' - this time it worked), which the production company had read and liked amusing. He invited me to come into their East London office to discuss a possible creative position on the show. I was questioned by Tim and Dilly, the thirtysomething, teeny-tiny, fresh-faced BAFTA-winning executive producers. They explained that they had seen my assessment of the final episode, which included some lighthearted recommendations to the show's creators on how to improve the next series. The company's owner, Dan, who rose to prominence in the 1990s as the producer and co-host of a phenomenally successful late-night chat show, had scoured the internet for reviews. When he found mine, he printed copies for all of the producers, who read it on their way to a meeting with the channel and, surprise, agreed with everything.

I left my first half-hour interview with Dilly and Tim feeling calm about the possibility of never hearing from them again. I had no idea what they were looking for, and we spent the majority of the session analyzing the habits of affluent people and psychoanalyzing the actors. We didn't really discuss my qualifications, employment history, or job requirements at all. I had no idea at the time that proper psychoanalysis accounts for 90% of good reality TV production. And my years of watching affluent people's behaviors while feeling on the outside of their club - standing in boarding school tuck shops and smoking areas of King's Road nightclubs - would, for once, overqualify me for a position.

I received a second call from the series producer three days later, while I was at a music festival with Leo. We had been appointed as our camping party's Official Glitter Appliers, a responsibility we gladly accepted. A boy high on acid heard incessant ringing emanating from my tent and assumed it was Kraftwerk performing a surprise set. It was, indeed, Dilly. She informed me that I had been hired as the show's story producer and that I should report for my first meeting the next day.

I arrived at work fresh from the festival, having not washed in four days, my nose sunburned, and my white-blonde pixie hair matted into a Mohawk. Leo waited in reception with our baggage and tent, while I attended my first story meeting. I'd run out of clean clothes, so I dressed in Leo's big T-shirt, laddered tights, and ballet pumps. The attire was a perfect send-off for my last day as a child and first day as an adult.

I fell in love with the inventiveness, fun, and relentlessness of my new career, my new colleagues, and my new employers almost as much as I did with Leo. When I wasn't in the office or on location, I started taking freelance journalistic jobs so I could write in the evenings and weekends, leaving me with little to no time for anything else, much to Leo's dismay. He felt little cheated. He had fallen in love with a rootless girl who wanted nothing more than to pack a bag of plimsolls and jeans and go on any adventure he took her on; she embroidered his initials into jumpers and spent the entire party locked in a bathroom with him, sitting in the empty bath, staring at his face with saucer-like eyes. He ended up with a woman who had a distinct adult identity and was preoccupied with her work.

I felt that our relationship had been one of the most fulfilling experiences of my life, and that he would always be an important part of who I had become, but we had outgrown each other. I realized I had to let him go so he could be with someone who truly wanted to be in a relationship and give him the love and devotion he deserved.

Farly, AJ, and I had finally moved out of our parents' suburban homes and into our first London home. AJ, too, had recently become single. Farley was still with Scott.

Part of me hoped that by living with two single women, Farly would realize what she had been missing in her twenties and end her relationship with Scott. But if anything, living with AJ and me made her appreciate him even more. She once watched me run about getting ready for a first date, trim some new fake eyelashes, apply them, and then scream in agony as I realized I had used the kitchen scissors I used to slice chillies over pizza the night before. She fetched a package of frozen potato smiley-face shapes and placed them over my eyes while I emailed the guy to cancel. 'God, I do not miss this,' she groaned.

When Scott was abroad on business, Farly, AJ, and I went dancing at our favorite Camden dive club. We returned home and opened an out-of-date bottle of Tia Maria, and things became confessional in the way they frequently do in the aftermath of a night out.

'I miss Scott,' Farly said after finishing the last of her Tia Maria.

'Why?' I exclaimed. AJ stared at me. 'I mean, he's only gone for a few days.

I understand, yet I still miss him while he's gone. I get aroused every time I see him. Even if he only goes to the corner shop and returns, I'm looking forward to hearing the front door open again. She noticed my frown. "I know it sounds cheesy, but it is true."

'I believe she truly loves him,' I said the next day.

'Of course she loves him,' AJ replied, lying on the sofa and chewing on a bacon sandwich. 'Why do you believe they have been together for three years?'

I don't know. I assumed she just wanted to know what having a boyfriend was like.'

AJ shook her head in surprise. 'Come on, Mate.'

After realizing this, I began to notice subtle signs everywhere. Scott's parents had met Farly's parents. Farly spent increasingly more weekends with his adult friends, doing grown-up things like 'thirtieth birthday weekends in the Cotswolds' and wine tasting on a weekday. Scott was around a lot, which I despised. I also disliked it when he wasn't present. He could not win. I did not want him to win.

THE UNCOOL GIRLS OF UNCOOL CAMDEN

When I was 24, in my first year of living in London with Farly and AJ, I went out for a drink with a friend on a Tuesday night after work. Despite my efforts to keep her out till last orders, she had to call it a night at half eight due to an early meeting the next morning. I texted everybody in my phonebook who I knew would be available and interested in spending the night with me, but everyone was either busy, in bed, or exhausted. I sulked onto the 24 bus home, my trusty steed that whisked me from the heart of London to right outside my door in twenty minutes, and felt restless and sad that I couldn't stay out for just one more hour and one more glass of wine. It was a feeling I grew accustomed to: panicked and throaty; a sense that everyone in London was having a good time except for me; that there were pots of experiential gold hidden on every street corner and I wasn't finding them; and that one day I would be dead, so why ruin a potentially perfect and glorious day with an early night?

I snapped out of my funk when the 24 arrived at a tavern at the end of my street. It was a NW5 hovel, a once-famous music venue turned gloomy boozer for the nine a.m. Camden residents who consume alcohol. I got off the bus and went inside. It was the first time I'd come since the day we moved in, when we were informed that Farly had made history by being the first customer in forty years to order coffee. The landlord walked across the street to the corner store to get some Nescafé Gold Blend and milk, charging her 26p.

I ordered a beer and made small chat with the bartender, who appeared unsurprised to be serving another lone drinker. A man in his late sixties with a grey yeti beard asked how my day had gone, and I bemoaned the fact that I didn't have a drinking friend to accompany me. He claimed he was the right man for the task. As we drank, he told me about his childhood in the area: the school he'd skipped, how things had changed, the drinking holes that had closed; the John Martyn concert he'd attended at the Camden Palace before I was born, the live recordings of which I had compulsively listened to. I departed at midnight, scrawling the man's phone number on the back of a beer mat with the mutual promise of spending the afternoon together listening to records, but knowing I'd never contact him again. He was simply 'a night', and I wished for many more. A recollection, an anecdote, a new face, or an experience. He was a piece of advice, a gossipy story, and an intriguing fact that became lodged in my inebriated, unconscious mind, only to be plucked out and regurgitated as my own one day. Where did you hear this? Somebody would ask. I would respond, "I have no idea."

The next evening, when I returned home from work with an unmovable hangover to find Farly and AJ snuggled up on the sofa, I told them how I wound up in a dirty pub down the road the night before.

'Why on Earth did you do that? AJ asked perplexedly.

'Because it was Tuesday night,' I answered. 'And I can.'

I am pleased that as a teenager, I fetishized the measured-out-in-coffee-spoons minutiae of maturity so vividly, since the relief of eventually arriving there meant I found very little of it to be burdensome. I've enjoyed paying my own rent. I've enjoyed cooking for myself every day. I used to get a thrill sitting in the doctor's waiting room, knowing I had registered and gotten myself there without the assistance of anyone else. In my first year of bill-paying, a letter from Thames Water addressed to me would practically make me weak in the knees. I would gladly accept the administrative burden of adulthood in exchange for the assurance that I may go to the pub on my own and make friends with an old man any day of the week.

To this day, I can't get over the fact that I no longer have to sip gin from shampoo bottles, that there is no lights-out, and that I can stay up until four a.m. watching movies or writing. If I wanted, I could do it on a weeknight. I'm relieved, motivated, and stimulated that I can eat breakfast for dinner, listen to loud music, and smoke a cigarette from my window. I still can't believe my luck. My entire life as a young twenty-something adult was spent like Macaulay Culkin in Home Alone 2: Lost in New York, when he finds himself booked at The Plaza and orders mountains and mountains of ice cream from room service while watching mafia flicks. I completely blame this on my rigid upbringing. Almost every adult I've encountered who attended boarding school couldn't believe they now live a life in which they can go to a Kentish Town old man's bar on a Tuesday night and not face a detention, suspension, or rustication, whatever that means. If university had been a playground for me to act out my grownup aspirations, having my own home and paycheck in London was akin to utopia.

We looked for three months before discovering our first adult London house. Our budget was limited, and flats with three double beds were difficult to find. There was a property in Finsbury Park that was cleverly photographed to look like a Notting Hill mews house but, upon arrival, we discovered looked more like a wing of Pentonville Prison. Farly and AJ went a catastrophic showing of a property on the estate in Brixton, along with a large throng of millennial aspirants who queued outside like it was Madame Tussaud's. The estate agent failed to bring the keys, so they had to wait for half an hour. When they eventually finished a three-minute tour of the dump and departed, they all had to drop down to the ground because a gunman was on the loose and being pursued by police outside the property. Finally, just when we were about to give up hope, Farly discovered a three-bedroom rental within our price range on Gumtree through a private landlord.

It was just off a notoriously unsafe crescent connecting Camden Town's Chalk Farm and Kentish Town ends. It had a true old-fashioned market twice a week that offered pairs of five-pound slippers and cartoon bed sheets; a daily fruit and vegetable stall; and a cash-only independent store that sold marijuana from under the sandwich counter. It was graceless, gaudy, and beautiful.

The house was a lovely mess. One of a row of 1970s ex-council maisonettes fashioned of Lego-yellow bricks with unusual window and door arrangement and proportions that gave the impression that it was created in a hurry by a teenager playing The Sims. In the summer, the front garden had two overgrown shrubs that made it impossible to get through the old wooden front gate without strenuous arm-swiping. The kitchen tiles were decorated with pictures of the English countryside. The back garden was overgrown with weeds. There were strange liquid streak streaks down the hallway wall that, after much investigation, we could only guess were pee. Everything smelled extremely moist. Squatters occupied the flat above us.

Gordon, the landlord, was a handsome man in his forties who wore a boxy midlife crisis leather jacket and had unusually dark, floppy hair. He was also a BBC news presenter, and he wanted everyone to know about it. His voice was loud and sophisticated, and his demeanor was strangely harsh and informal.

'So, this is the hallway,' Gordon exclaimed. 'As you can see, there's plenty of storage space.' We unlocked one of the enormous dusty white doors. A black box labeled 'RAT ATTACK!' lay in the center of the vacant shelves.' printed across it in bold yellow font. 'Oh, disregard that,' he murmured, sweeping it up with his palm. 'All sorted now.' We exchanged short glances. 'Do you know what?He crinkled his nose slightly as he stated this. 'I think the best thing is that I'll just get out of your way and let you explore the location yourself. Tell me when you have seen everything.

It was quirky, wobbly, and weird, but we knew it was the ideal first home not only for us, but also for our extended family of friends, whom we planned to invite over every weekend. We walked back downstairs to tell Gordon we wanted it, but he was on the phone.

"Ya... ya... well." "That's the worst-case scenario," he replied, dismissively waving his hand at us. 'Ya. For the time being, let us try to avoid going to court. I don't want to go back there AGAIN.' He looked at us and rolled his eyes. 'Great, I'll be around tomorrow at ten to see this roof. OK. Yap. Okay. Yes, yes. OK. 'Bye.' He tucked his phone into his jeans' back pocket. 'Bloody tenants,' he declared. So, do you want it or not?'

We scrimped and saved to meet our deposits, so the first month was spent living in an exhilarating, crazy, frenetic frugal lifestyle. We didn't have much for the house, so Farly bought a pack of Post-its to attach on various surfaces and write stuff like 'TV WILL BE HERE' or 'TOASTER WILL BE HERE'. Every night, we had Marmite and cucumber sandwiches for dinner. On the second night in our new home, I arrived to find both girls running around the living room in their wellies, having discovered the first mouse and not wanting it to run over their bare feet as they attempted to catch it. Farly purchased a block of Pilgrims Choice Cheddar from the Nisa Local, placed it in her empty vanity case, and waggled it around the carpet, hoping to coax the mouse to a safe rescue.

We also quickly became acquainted with the manager of the neighborhood corner shop, a middle-aged man named Ivan who was built like a marine. On our initial visit, he warned us that if we 'came into any trouble with any gangs', we should come to him right away because it would be 'dealt with'. Farley was wearing a strand of pearls at the time. But I felt strangely safer knowing Ivan was always a ten-second walk from our front door, and when the mouse problem became a recurring issue, he was always there to help. I'd often jump out of the home barefoot in pyjamas and into the shop, shouting, 'IT'S BACK, IVAN!' IT IS BACK!' with a Blanche DuBois-like frenzy.

"All right, dahlin'," he would say. 'I'll come now. Would you like me to bring my gun?'I'd decline, ask him to bring his torch instead, and he'd crouch under every bed, fridge, and sofa to look for it.

(Eventually, Gordon organized for an exterminator to come in, an East End geezer with the surname 'Mouser'. When he laid down some traps, I asked him whether there was a more humane way of dealing with the problem.

'No,' he replied, his arms folded in dismay.

'OK,' I responded, 'it's only that I'm vegetarian.'

He said, "Well, you don't have to eat it."

Camden seemed like the appropriate place for us to be: it was central, close to all the best parks, and, most of all, it was dangerously, hopelessly uncool. None of our friends lived there, and no one our age did. When we walked out on Camden High Street, we were welcomed with swarms of Spanish students on a school trip or forty-something men with Paul Weller hairstyles and winkle-picker shoes who were still hoping for Camden's glory years of Britpop to return. AJ used to call it "Goon Watch." We'd walk down High Street on a Saturday night, and she'd slur 'Goon, goon, goon' in my ear while pointing at passers-by. For the first few months I lived there, I had a gorgeous but ultimately ruinously self-obsessed musician lover who lived in East London and refused to pay me visits since Camden was 'too 2007'.

Occasionally, during our time there, we'd go to a party or a night out in East London and be surrounded by young, cool, beautiful people, wondering if this was truly where we were supposed to be at our age. However, as we left, we were usually weary by the experience and thankful that we lived somewhere where we didn't have to pretend to be cooler than we were, which was not very cool. We could go shopping in our leggings and hoodies, no bra, and not run into anyone we knew. We could take over a dance floor and perform a drunken, hilarious cancan in a line while still being the coolest people in the place. We could go out and spend the entire evening engaged in one other, without attempting to impress anyone. There simply wasn't anyone left in Camden to impress.

One of the first items I purchased for the home was an industrial-sized cooking pot suitable for a soup kitchen. Our friends had always enjoyed eating together, and I was overjoyed to have my own stove and kitchen table. We held dinner parties three times a week throughout our first year of living together. I calculated the cheapest things to make: pot after pot of dhal, tray after tray of Parmigiana. In the summer, we'd have candlelit dinners in our terribly overgrown yard, which had become so overgrown that a tree caught fire in a strangely biblical manner, and we all drunkenly splashed saucepans of water and glasses of Ivan's terrible five-pound Sauvignon Blanc over it.

There was a liberation in the realization that our house was fundamentally too broken to repair. Gordon was also unconcerned; he let us paint all of the walls brilliant colors and never reacted when the paint stopped with a wavering line on the stairway wall, indicating that we had reached the bottom of the Dulux tin. It meant it was a house we could actually live in, not one we were very attached to. We could ruin it on a Saturday night, and all it would take was a ten-minute clean-up the next morning to make it seem decent again. We could play our record player at full blast till six a.m. without the neighbors complaining - I swear those 1970s houses were designed to be disco-proof, because we never received a single noise complaint in the years we lived there. In fact, the neighbour said she had never heard us. As a result, our residence became a gathering place for people looking to get high.

I got the majority of my drug experimenting out of my system during my first few years in London. First, I developed a familial relationship with Fergus, a pleasant drug dealer. Fergus wasn't the type to sit in the car and pass you a baggie under the dashboard; instead, he'd join me late on a Friday night when I had friends over for dinner, rolling spliffs at the table and telling long-winded jokes while digging into the leftovers, before I'd finally send him packing with a Tupperware box of spaghetti carbonara. Farly, who had always been much more sensible than me and was always in bed by midnight when we had guests over for supper, had never met Fergus but was always perplexed by the way I spoke about him as if he were 'a cousin or a family acquaintance'. She awoke at 4:00 a.m. one night. by the sound of me giving Fergus an estate agent's walking tour of the house while advising him on the feng shui of each room. The next day, Mom walked into my room and found me huffing and puffing as I moved my bed to the opposite wall.

What are you doing?' she inquired.

'I am shifting my bed. Fergus claims it is not in a good situation at the time.

'Why?'

'Because the headboard is too close to the radiator. He claims that being around heat is bad for your head, particularly your sinuses.

'Yeah, Dolly, the man sells you Class A drugs,' Farly explained. 'He's in no position to give health advice.'

Fergus abruptly dropped out of contact, as I was warned they sometimes do, so I was directed to CJ, who was a steadfast catastrophe. CJ was known as London's worst drug dealer. His timekeeping was horrible; he would frequently give the 'wrong order' to the 'wrong client' and then show up at your door half an hour later, begging for the 'stuff' back. His phone was never recharged. His satellite navigation system was constantly failing. He had kept me waiting for an hour and a half, and I found myself telling him on the phone that he was 'his own worst enemy', like a furious teacher. The final straw came on the Thursday before I left London to attend a festival, when I called him to ask if he could sell me some MDMA.

'What is that?' he asked.

'MDMA,' I responded. 'Mandy.'

'Who is she?'

'Ecstasy. Come on. MDMA.'

'I've never heard of that,' he replied.

Regardless of how or who I obtained them from, the purchase of drugs was almost always more exciting than the substance itself. Talking about getting some, contacting the number, withdrawing the cash; someone waiting in the flat while someone else went to get the car, returning with a tiny plastic pocket of herbs or powder; the promise of what was to follow - that was the part that had my heart racing the fastest. Farly once witnessed the work required to purchase, split, and consume cocaine, and she couldn't believe how time-consuming it was; 'Like making a shepherd's pie,' she observed. But the time-consuming faff of lining up powder and rolling up spliffs is what makes it so enjoyable for someone who never wants a night to end - it's a distraction, a guaranteed night extension. It's the muting of your sensible thinking that says, "Go to bed at eleven, we've talked about everything we could possibly want to talk about now," and replaces it with an artificial desire for the party to go on forever. For me, cocaine was always just a way to keep drinking and staying awake long after I was exhausted; I was never particularly fond of any sensation it provided.

I believed that in order to be a writer, I needed to accumulate experiences. And I used to believe that every worthwhile event and person could only be found after nightfall. I've always remembered something Hicks told me while we lay in bed, the fairy lights of her student room glittering around her window.

'One day, Dolly, we shall sit in a nursing home, bored out of our minds and staring at the quilt on our laps,' she lamented. 'And all we'll have to grin about are these memories.'

However, as these nights became more frequent, I began to feel identified by these stories rather than as an expert collector. Staying out until dawn became a regular occurrence, and I grew to associate any evening out with a hedonistic all-nighter. Worse, everyone else expected the same thing from me. A night with me meant a night that would wreck you for the next day, and friends expected the same level of debauchery from me, even when we met up for a fast pad thai on a Thursday night. My energies, bank account, and mental state could not keep up with it. And I didn't want to self-mythologize and inflate myself into this terrible Village Drunk figure with whom everyone would avoid organizing a coffee date, knowing that it would most likely end the next morning in some all-night casino in Leicester

Square.

'I adore those stories,' Helen said one morning after we'd been to a party and I'd collected a gathering of people to bore them with my best folkloric tales of nights out. 'But there are quite a few of them, doll.'

Another thing no one tells you about drinking as you get older is that it's not the hangovers that become crushing, but the severe paranoia and dread in the sober hours of the next day, which became a regular part of my mid-twenties. The gap between who you were on a Saturday night, commandeering an entire pub garden by shouting obnoxiously about how you've always felt you had at least three prime-time sitcom scripts in you, and who you are on a Sunday afternoon, thinking about death and wondering if the postman likes you or not, becomes too large. Growing up promotes self-awareness. And self-awareness is a death sentence for a self-proclaimed party girl. I also ended up having two completely different jobs: working in television and as a freelance writer. They needed more and more of my time and attention, and frequent blackout boozing and hangovers were detrimental to productivity and creativity. "You're trying to live two lives," a buddy once told me when I was on the verge of fatigue. 'You have to decide if you want to be the woman who works harder than anyone else or the woman who parties harder.'

I choose to aim for the latter. Life became more fulfilling during the day, and there was less of a need to flee at night. But it would take me some time to discover that the path to adventure is not limited to late nights, hot pubs, cold wine, strangers' flats, parked cars with lights on, and small bags of powder. I'd always thought of alcohol as a means of transporting experience, but as I got older, I realized it had the same capacity to stunt as it did to intensify it. Sure, there were the juicy confessionals from folks with dilated pupils in a lavatory cubicle; the old men with good stories you'd never meet otherwise; the locations you'd go; and the people you'd kiss. But there was also all the work that you couldn't complete when hungover. All the negative impressions you'd create on potential friends because you were so intoxicated you couldn't speak. All those lost discussions in which someone tells you something extremely significant, but neither of you remembers it the next morning. All those hours spent laying in your bed at 5 a.m., sweating and panicking, your heart racing as you stare at the ceiling, frantically wanting to sleep. All the hours lost in the cul-de-sac of your mind torturing yourself with all the idiotic things you said and did, hating yourself for the next several days.

Years later, I discovered that consistently behaving in a way that makes you feel ashamed means you can't take yourself seriously, and your self-esteem plummets. Ironically, my teenage one-woman crusade to become an adult through excessive drinking left me feeling more like a child than any other action I've taken in my life. For years of my twenties, I wandered around feeling as if I was about to be accused of something dreadful, as if someone might easily march up to me and scream, 'YOU'RE the dick who drank Jo Malone Pear and Freesia bath oil in a pint glass at my house party for a dare - you owe me £42!'"; or 'OI! TOSS THE POT! I still can't believe you left with my boyfriend outside the Mornington Crescent Sainsbury's!' - and I'd have to nod solemnly and say, 'Yes, I can't recollect it particularly, but I'll take your word for it and I'm sorry.' Imagine walking about in a world where you believe someone is ALWAYS about to tell you you're an arsehole, and you're ready to agree wholeheartedly. What kind of fun is that?

Wherever I am on a Tuesday night, from now until the day I die, you can bet I would rather be in a dismal pub in Camden, sipping beer and talking to a stranger. But I finally grew out of those clockwork-regular blackout benders that wiped out the next day like a tsunami, just as I grew out of the deteriorating yellow-bricked maisonette. For a little period of time, however, sitting in my overgrown Eden garden, drinking sour Sauvignon with the people I loved, the record player turned up loud, and the empty plates heaped high by the sink, I thought I lived in the nicest house ever. I still believe I did.

'NOTHING WILL CHANGE'

One of my least favorite aspects of Farly meeting Scott was that I never saw her family again. I missed her mother, father, stepmother, brother, and sister. For years, I spent every other weekend and holiday with her family, and they felt like my own. But after Scott came on the picture, Farly stopped calling me up, and I only saw them once or twice a year. Scott now sat at the dining-room table where I had previously sat for birthdays and Sunday roasts; he was the one who accompanied them on chilly, pleasant autumnal half-terms in

Cornwall while I browsed Instagram.

After a few months in our new London home, Farly invited me out for a walk with her family one Saturday afternoon. We stopped at a pub for lunch, and I reveled in the warm familiarity of their rituals: nicknames, inside jokes, and stories about Farly and me as teenagers. I felt arrogant; whatever space Scott had been occupying for the past few years was not the same as mine, because nothing had changed.

We fell behind the rest of the party and the dog on the final section of the walk, like we had as youths, due to competitive over-eating at lunch.

'Scott has asked me to move in with him.

'What did you say?' I inquired.

'I'm going to do it,' she whispered almost regretfully, her timid words drifting into the frigid air. "It felt right when he asked me."

'When?'

'After I've spent a year with you people in Camden,' she responded. I despised the expression 'done a year' as if I were a gap-year ski season or a TEFL course in Japan, something you do once for an entertaining anecdotal story.

'OK,' I responded.

'I'm very sorry; I know it's really difficult.'

'No, no, I'm pleased for you,' I replied. We finished the rest of the hike in quiet.

Do you want to bake chocolate chip cookies? Farly said as we returned to our residence.

'Yeah.'

'Great. Make a list of everything we need, and I'll go get the stuff. And why don't we watch Joni Mitchell's documentary, which has been sitting on the shelf for ages?

'Sure,' I replied. It brought back memories of when I was eight years old and my mother took me to McDonald's after my goldfish died.

We sat on the sofa munching cookies, our legs entangled and our tummies protruding from our pyjamas. Graham Nash was discussing the soul-baring lyrics of Blue.

'I know every single word on that album,' I stated. When Farly passed her driving test at the age of seventeen, we had only brought one album with us on a three-week summer road trip.

'Me, too. "Carey" is my favorite.'

"All I want" is mine. I paused to finish my cookie and remove the crumbs from my mouth. 'We'll probably never do a road trip like that again.'

'Why?'

'Because you're moving in with your boyfriend, you'll be doing all your road trips with him now.'

'Do not be dumb,' she added. 'Nothing will change.'

I'd like to take a moment to discuss 'nothing will change'. I've had it told to me several times by women I love in their twenties when they move in with boyfriends, get engaged, move abroad, marry, and become pregnant. 'Nothing will change.' It drives me crazy. Everything will change. Everything will change. The affection we have for each other remains constant, but the format, tone, frequency, and intimacy of our connection will change forever.

You remember when you were a teenager and you saw your mother with her best friends, and they appeared to be close, but they weren't like you and your pals? When they first met, there was a peculiar formality between them, a sense of unease. Your mother would tidy the house before they arrived, and they would discuss their children's coughs and hairstyles. Farly once told me as a kid, 'Promise we'll never get like that. Promise that when we are fifty, we will be exactly the same. I want us to sit on the sofa, filling our cheeks with crackers and discussing thrush. I don't want to become one of those women who only get together every few months for a craft expo at the NEC. I promised. But I had no idea how hard it is to maintain that level of intimacy with a friend as you get older; it does not happen by chance.

I've seen it time and again: a woman always fits into a man's life better than he does into hers. She will be the one who spends the most time at his apartment, and she will be the one who meets all of his friends and their girlfriends. She will be the one who brings flowers to his mother on her birthday. Women dislike this rigmarole just as much as men do, but they are better at it; they simply get on with it.

This means that when a lady my age falls in love with a man, the list of priorities goes as follows:

1. Family
2. Friends

To this:

1. Family
2. Boyfriend
3. Boyfriend's family

4. Boyfriend's friends
5. Girlfriends of the boyfriend's friends
6. Friends

On average, you move from seeing your friend every weekend to once every six weekends. She becomes a baton, and you are at the absolute end of the track. You have your turn for, say, your birthday or brunch, and then you have to send her back to the boyfriend to begin the long, dull rotation again.

These gaps in each other's lives gradually but steadily build a chasm in the heart of your connection. The affection is still present, but the familiarity is not. Before you realize it, you are no longer living together. You're living your lives apart with your men, then getting together for supper every six weekends to share your experiences. I now see why our mothers cleaned the home before their best friend arrived and asked, 'What's the news, then?' in a cheerful, stilted manner. I understand how that happens.

So don't tell me that after you move in with your lover, nothing will change. There will be no road trip; the cycle also applies to holidays: I'll see my pal every sixth summer, unless she has a baby, in which case I'll have my road trip in eighteen years. It never stops happening. Everything will change.

Farly moved out on my 25th birthday. She and Scott found a one-bedroom flat with a roof terrace to rent in Kilburn. It was opposite a gym, which they claimed was ideal because they enjoyed badminton. She made a point of showing me that there was a direct bus from Camden to Kilburn High Road. I sulked on the way to their housewarming drinks.

I spent the party chain smoking on the roof terrace, with Farly's teenage sister, Florence, sitting on my lap and showing me her yearbook. Later, when I was intoxicated, I told her that I secretly hoped one of them was unfaithful or Scott was gay, so Farly would have to move back into our home. She giggled and hugged me.

'I detest that,' Farly muttered, pointing to a framed Manchester United shirt covered in the team's signatures and hanging in the hall, sensing I needed something to vent my frustrations on.

'Yeah, it's dreadful,' I responded.

'Rank,' she answered. Living with a boy. Urgh.'

'Girls are so much more enjoyable to live with.

'The best.' She smiled. Do you like the flat?'

'I just love it. I think you'll be really happy here." And, annoyingly, I finally believed it.

Our university buddy Belle, who arrived with a guitar and a desire to go dancing all weekend, went into Farly's room, and life continued as usual. The refrigerator still leaked. The downstairs loo continued to remain broken. Gordon still barged uninvited into our house on Saturday mornings, attempting to dump horrible pieces of furniture on us as a 'gift' since he couldn't be bothered to take them to the rubbish. We still did something called 'ladies' choice' when one of us went to the store, which meant you got whichever chocolate bar they bring back. At first, I saw Farly more than I had when we were living together, just because she was so concerned with making me feel like 'nothing' had changed. But I soon saw less of her. Everything changed.

Three months after they moved in together, I was sitting at my desk at work when I noticed on my phone that Scott had invited me to join a WhatsApp group called 'Exciting News'.

I knew what it was and didn't open it. I had been waiting for this moment since Farly informed me that they were moving in together. I wasn't ready to know, so I kept working as if it was all just a recurring dream, an unsent mail in the ether's inbox. My phone remained on my desk for an hour, with the notification starring at me.

Finally, I received a call from AJ, who had also been invited to the group, and she instructed me to open it. It stated that he was suggesting. Valentines Day. Four years since their first date. He asked if we might gather a group of her friends and surprise her in a pub once he'd done it. I responded I would love to. I stated I couldn't wait. I stated I was over the moon.

I cried, knowing I had lost whatever battle I was fighting with whatever I was attempting to fight against.

Dilly walked by.

'Dollbird,' she announced. What's going on?'

I mumbled, 'Nothing'.

'Come on.' She took my hand and led me to the boardroom. 'Tell me what's going on.' I informed her about the proposal. She was familiar with the story, having met Farly several times and been captivated by the Scott-Farly-Dolly love triangle for years, describing it as 'the perfect structured reality tale'.

'And I know I sound theatrical,' I added between sobs. 'I know people grow up and things change, but I never expected everything to change when we were just twenty-five.' She glanced at me and sighed, shaking her head regretfully.

'What?' I asked.

'I always knew we should have rigged the place with cameras when you moved into that house,' she remarked, rolling her eyes. 'I knew it; I mentioned it to Dave at the time. I realize you don't want to appear on camera, but this could have been a great series arc.'

I gathered our buddies and informed them Scott's plan. We planned a time and location where we would be waiting with a present. I purchased them a framed poster from Etsy with the lyrics to their favourite Smiths song, 'There Is A Light That Never Goes Out'. AJ offered to purchase me the 'Heaven Knows I'm Miserable Now' one.

I'd never desired any of it. I never wanted her to spend every weekend with Scott's friends and their wives at bloody Balham barbecues. I did not want to see her for catch-up dinners. I did not want her to move out after a year. I did not want her to get married. The worst part was that it was entirely my fault. If only I could have gone back in time and avoided setting them up. I never dated Hector. Never returned to Hector's on that snowy night in Notting Hill. I hoped I could go back and ignore him when he began talking to me on the train. I wished I had never boarded that filthy train in the first place.

The issue with having a Farly in your life is that their tale feels like your own. She wasn't living the life I had imagined for us, and I was grieving for the future I now knew we'd never have. Up until Scott, we were sticking to the plan: we went to the same institution, selected to live in the same halls, and then stayed in the same house for two years. When we graduated, I expected to have 'The London Years', not 'The London Year'. I expected to see several residences, not just one. I imagined we'd spend hundreds of nights out together that ended at morning. I expected gigs, double dates, excursions to European towns, and weeks spent stretched out on the beach together. I thought we could claim each other's twenties before having to give the other one up. I felt like Scott had taken our tale away from me. He had snatched ten years that were mine.

A month before Scott proposed, a number of us went out for drinks with Farly on Saturday night.

'Scott mentioned something unusual to me this week,' she revealed. We had already chipped in for the Smiths print and cleared Valentine's Day, so we covertly gazed at each other with blinking, bug-wide eyes.

'Go ahead,' I answered solemnly.

'He claimed he has a Valentine's Day surprise for me that is both little and large. And, I know it seems strange, but a part of me wondered if it was an engagement ring?'

'I don't think it's that,' Lacey remarked abruptly, avoiding all of us strained gazes, the mere meeting of which would undoubtedly give the game away.

'No, I understand. You're correct; it won't be,' Farly answered hastily, with a self-effacing giggle.

'Yeah,' AJ replied. "I think you're reading into it too much, dude."

'What could be both little and large? I can't figure out what it is,' Farly replied.

'Oh, I don't know,' Lacey replied. 'Maybe plane tickets for a vacation or something?'

'Perhaps it's a dog collar,' I replied frankly.

'What?' she inquired.

'That is a minor yet significant issue. Perhaps he's decided to become a clergyman and wishes to inform you on your anniversary.

'Oh, Dolly, stop it.' Farly sighed.

'Or maybe …maybe,' I muttered, my mouth catching up with the liter of white wine I had consumed. Perhaps he has opted to have a Manchester United tattoo on his face. It appears small, but it is actually rather large, isn't it? It might influence your feelings about him.' AJ signaled for me to stop with a modest throat-slitty motion. 'Or maybe it's the keys to a boat; perhaps he's purchased a speedboat for the Thames. A significant lifestyle shift, especially if he wants to take it out on weekends. I guess it is pretty costly to maintain. Perhaps that's it. He is a seafaring guy, but he has never found the opportunity to tell you.

'I don't want to guess what it is anymore,' Farly exclaimed.

I couldn't sleep the night before the engagement, thinking about how Farly's life was going to change in ways she had no idea. I texted Scott the next morning, 'Good luck tonight. I know you'll ace it. I hope she says yes. If not, it's been a pleasure knowing you x.

'Thank you for your message of confidence, Dolls x,' he answered.

We sat at the bar together, waiting for Scott's text.

What if she says no?AJ asked. Do we just go home?'

'She won't say no,' I said. 'But if she does, I've already checked out what else is going on and there's a disco night at KOKO, so we just head there for a dance - it's ten quid on the door.'

Scott texted me at ten to say they were engaged. He'd told her they were going for one last celebration drink before heading home. We got a bottle of champagne, poured them two glasses, and glanced out the window while waiting for their taxi. Finally, we watched them go into the bar, and AJ gripped my sweaty palm twice, sending the silent universal Morse code.

'CONGRATULATIONS!We all cheered when Farly went through the door. She glanced at us in complete disbelief, then at Scott. He smiled at her, and she ran up to me for a hug.

"Congratulations," I replied, handing Scott his glass of champagne. 'You have made my best friend really happy.'

'I am so delighted you dated that idiot Hector,' he remarked, chuckling. I love you, Dolly.

His eyes filled with tears, and he hugged me.

I wondered if he understood how I was feeling. I wondered if he had always known. Perhaps that's why he sought to include me on the night they got engaged, gave me my own project, and otherwise involved me.

Two hours later, Farly had asked me to be her maid of honor, I had consumed the majority of their celebratory champagne, and I was feeling talkative.

'I wanna make a speech,' I slurred at AJ, picking up a fork to tap on my glass.

'No, dear,' AJ said, taking the fork away from me and pointing to the other girls, who quickly removed all of the cutlery from the table and handed it to the waiter. 'No speech.'

'But I am her fuckin' maid of honour.'

'I know, darling, but there will be plenty of time for speeches.' When AJ used the restroom, I crawled beneath the table and discovered her car keys in her handbag. I clinked them against the glass with a ding ding ding.

'When I initially learned that Scott and Farly were engaged, I was furious,' I said.

'Oh God,' Belle moaned.

'Because I've known this little freak for almost twenty-five years.'

'Over 25 years?Lacey asked Hicks.

'SHUDUP!' I cried, pointing at Lacey, my wine falling on the table.

'THIS IS SHIT; YOU ARE NO LONGER A MAID OF HONOUR!'

Farly shouted drunkenly across the table.

'But when I look about, I see that the world -' I paused for dramatic effect - 'is just how it should be. My best friend has won the best man.'

'Awww,' everyone exclaimed with a simultaneous exhale of relief.

'To Scott and Farly,' I said through tears, sitting down. Everyone gave a feeble round of applause.

'Beautiful,' Belle whispered to me, 'even though I know you got that from Julia Roberts' speech in My Best Friend's Wedding.'

'Oh, she won't know,' I snarled and waved my hand dismissively.

To this day, the rest of that evening seems like a blur. I invited Dilly and her husband, who were in the region to celebrate Valentine's Day, to join us. I did the cancan in the bar's dining area while singing 'One' from A Chorus Line and high-kicked a tray of plates right out of a waiter's hands, crushing it to bits on the floor. I said my goodbyes to Scott and Farly before returning to my Camden flat and forcing everyone to continue drinking till six a.m. I awoke next to a semi-clothed Hicks who had scrawled happy Valentine's Day on her breasts with wet eyeliner.

I spent the next day on social media, monitoring Farly's 'engagement weekend' (I don't want to be too careful about this particular detail, but I believed one evening would suffice). There was a family BBQ, lunch at the Wolseley, and Scott's friends and their spouses showering her with gifts such as Smythson wedding planner notebooks and magnums of champagne, making my framed print appear quite little. I started feeling like the fourth, forgotten Wise Man (who had brought a piece of tat from Etsy).

'I believe you found Friday night rather overwhelming,' Farly replied over the phone. 'Are you okay?'

I'm fine! I'm not sure what you mean by "overwhelming". I mean, I am not the one who got engaged. You were the one who seemed overwhelmed. I saw on Facebook that Michelle purchased you the Smythson wedding planning book; isn't that nice?'

'Do you want to go out to supper next week, just the two of us?'

'Sure.'

I emailed Hector for the first time in four years.

Remember me? Scott and Farley are getting married. Thank goodness you sent me down to your kitchen without clothing on.

He responded. He claimed he had seen the news on Facebook. He informed me he had quit the City for travel PR and had a huge expense account, and he asked if he could take me out for a boozy lunch to celebrate our matchmaking skills. I believed we were the thin end of the'matchmakers' wedge, but I said yes because I was feeling down. In a moment of forced nostalgia, I scoured my inbox for all of his previous nasty poetry. I cancelled lunch the day before it occurred.

Why do you think you emailed him?' Farly inquired between bites of her burger at dinner a few days later.

I don't know. I believe I just want a boyfriend.

'Really?She asked, wiping her mouth with her tissue. 'You keep saying you don't want one.'

'Yeah, but I've been feeling weird recently.'

What sparked it?'

What sparked it? I was jealous. This time, however, I was jealous of Farly rather than Scott.

'You are getting engaged.'

'Why?' she inquired.

'Because I despise how different your life is today from mine. I hate that we used to do things together and now we don't.' I groaned. 'I hate that our children are so far apart in age. I detest that you're preparing to buy a flat with a man, while I had to beg my landlord to let me pay my rent three weeks late this month. I despise that you go about in Scott's Audi, which he was given from work, while I am still unable to drive. I despise the fact that his buddies are so different from mine, and I'm afraid they'll take you away because their lifestyles resemble your new life while mine do not. I know that seems mad, but it's not about me, and I'm destroying your beautiful time when I should be thrilled for you. But I feel so far behind you, and I'm afraid you'll run out of sight.

'If you had met your husband when you were twenty-two, I would have found it quite difficult,' she said.

'Really?'

Of course! I'd have despised it.

'Because sometimes I feel like I'm going insane.

'You are not mad. I'd have felt exactly the same. But I didn't choose to meet Scott when I was twenty-two. I was not seeking for a husband.'

'Yeah,' I said halfheartedly.

'And I will be there to enjoy and experience all of your life's milestones, whether they occur next month or in twenty years.'

'More like forty years,' I muttered. 'I still do not reside in a flat with curtains.'

'We are no longer at school. Stuff will happen at various times. You'll be doing things ahead of me, too.

Like, what? Meth?'

So, I eventually made peace with Scott. I understood he was not going anywhere. I spent time with each of them and resumed my usual and well-received role as Official Third Wheel. It's an unpleasant typecasting, but I do it extremely well. Only a little portion of my life has been spent in a relationship. I am The Threewheelin' Dolly Alderton, and I am well-versed and experienced in third-wheeling.

I spent my entire adolescence hanging around with my pals and their boyfriends. Smiling along while they wrestled on the couch or pretending to play snake on my phone while they slept in a corner of the room. I know how to smile and pretend with couples; in my twenties, I spent most weekday evenings around a table doing just that. I let them have phony disagreements in front of me about who gets to load or empty the dishwasher. I giggle as they recount extensive anecdotes about each other's sleeping habits. I remain silent as they discuss details of people's lives I've never heard of in an overly animated manner ('No WAY?! Priya didn't end up buying those tiles! I don't BELIEVE it! After all that! Oh God, sorry, explain to Dolly who Priya is and the entire story of the loft conversion from start to finish') to demonstrate that they have a wildly interesting life that does not involve me. And all the while, I pretend I don't understand why I'm the third wheel, doing all of the laughing and listening. But, of course, I know I'm just an aphrodisiac in their game of Domestic Bliss; I know when I leave, they'll rip each other's clothes off after an extended joint discourse about their holiday in the Philippines, especially since they both said the same island when I asked them what their favorite part was. I'm just a reluctant audience member.

But I still sit and watch all of these shows because the alternative, losing my friends, is not an option.

And when Farly and Scott weren't doing Their Bit on me, I realized, to my surprise, that Scott and I got along rather well. In fact, I hated not realizing this sooner since I would have liked his company when he was there while Farly and I lived together rather than just growling at him. He was both hilarious and smart. He read the article and formed opinions on several issues. Scott turned out to be a really nice man, and it was evident to me in retrospect that Farly would have chosen to marry someone wonderful. It was something I got completely incorrect.

When I wasn't busy helping Farly arrange her wedding, I tried to spend more time with his buddies. Whenever I had met them in the past, I had put on a huge, embarrassed show of establishing my differences from them. I got exceedingly intoxicated at a Sunday meal at our place once and lectured everyone on the'meat is murder' concept while they ate their roast lamb. In a pub, I accused one of his pals of being a sexist after he made a comment about my height. But after Farly and Scott got engaged, I did my best to relax, be pleasant, and get to know them. They were, after all, the people she spent the most of her time with now. They had to be half-interesting.

And then, on a Friday evening in August, we all stopped thinking about the wedding. Florence, Farly's 18-year-old sister, has been diagnosed with leukemia. 'Life is on hold,' Farly's father repeated over the months that followed. Life was on hold. The wedding was pushed back a year. Florence was a bridesmaid, and they wanted to make sure she was healthy enough by the time it came around. I'd spent months stressing about the wedding, and suddenly I couldn't care less.

Farly celebrated her twenty-seventh birthday a month after being diagnosed. We wanted to celebrate with her to take her mind off Florence's condition, but she was exhausted after spending every possible hour at the hospital. She didn't want to drink, she didn't want to be in a large crowd, and she didn't want to have to talk to so many people about how she was feeling. Her family couldn't come since they were camped out at the hospital. Scott decided that AJ and I would go over to their new flat, and he would make dinner for all four of us.

Farly's eleventh birthday was the first one we celebrated together. She has blown out more birthday candles with me than alone. I remember the first one like it was yesterday, when she was just a friend who sat next to me in math class. She donned a pink Miss Selfridge outfit, and we danced the Macarena in Bushey church hall.

But this birthday was unlike any other we'd had together. Farly was smaller than I had ever seen her, as little and frail as a newborn bird. There was no wild hugging or binge drinking. We were all quiet and gentle, especially Scott.

He had gotten up early to go to the fishmonger because AJ and I had quit eating meat. He prepared the most gorgeous sea bass stuffed with fennel and oranges, served with roast new potatoes, and presented it with the bitten-tongue concentration of a MasterChef contestant. He kissed Farly's head every time he walked by her. He held Farly's hand beneath the table. I saw the man she was in love with.

I texted Scott in the kitchen to let him know I had a tray of birthday cupcakes hidden behind the sofa. We waited for Farly to use the restroom, and AJ trapped her in with a chair while I frantically scattered the cakes on a tray and Scott looked for a box of matches.

'What's going on?!Farly yelped.

'In one minute!' I exclaimed as Scott and I lighted all of the candles.

We sung her 'Happy Birthday' and gave her her gifts and card. She blew out the candles and giggled as the three of us wrapped her in a large group hug.

Why did it take so long?' she inquired. Did you bake those while I was taking a piss? I was in there for so long that I began doing my thigh exercises.'

'Which thigh exercises?AJ asked.

'Oh, these new lunges I've heard about.' She began leaning up and down, some of her old, brilliant color dripping down her face. 'I try to do them each morning. I don't think it's making a difference. My legs still look like enormous gammon joints.' AJ began to imitate her, bobbing up and down stiffly, guided by Farly like a Rosemary Conley film.

Scott peered across the room and drew my attention. He grinned and said, 'Thanks,' mouthing it. I grinned back at him, suddenly realizing the universe that lay between us. The invisible dimension formed by the history, love, and future we shared with this single individual. I realized everything had changed: we had transitioned. We had not selected each other. But we were a family.

THE BAD DATE DIARIES: A £300 RESTAURANT BILL

It's December 2013, and I'm on my third date with an attractive entrepreneur I met through Tinder. He is the first wealthy man I've ever dated, and I'm terribly conflicted about him spending money on me. When he graciously picks up the tab, I feel flattered, as if this is how grownup courtship should operate. In other instances, I'm frustrated with myself for acting so predictably weak-kneed about an older man with a fast car and a drinking problem offering me champagne. This manifests itself in uncontrollable rage at him.

'You cannot own me!' I yell for no reason in the Mayfair restaurant he has selected, three bottles of wine to the good. 'I'm not a possession for you to own, and I won't feel obligated to dress up just so you can buy me some lobster! I can purchase it myself!

'Fine, darling, purchase it yourself,' he murmurs.

I will! I squawk. 'And not going Dutch, the whole thing.'

The waitress approaches with the bill for £300.

I walk to the lavatory to text my flatmate, AJ, and ask her to lend me £200 and transfer cash to my account immediately.

THE BAD PARTY CHRONICLES: MY HOUSE IN CAMDEN, CHRISTMAS, 2014

I've been pushing for a Rod Stewart-themed party since we moved into our Camden home two and a half years ago. In my opinion, Rod Stewart as a concept bridges the gap between the extreme campiness of Christmas and the carefree joie de vivre of a twenty-something house party.

My flatmates, Belle and AJ, reluctantly agree that our Christmas drinks party would be Rod Stewart-themed, but they insist on no accountability.

In the run-up to the party, I both prematurely age and bankrupt myself by searching for Rod Stewart-themed souvenirs. We have Rod Stewart-themed plastic cups, ashtrays, mince pies with sugar paper Rod Stewart faces, a life-size Rod Stewart cardboard cut-out, a Rod Stewart sign indicating where the loo is, and a Rod Stewart banner with the words MERRY CHRISTMAS, BABY!! on it. Sabrina, India, Farly, Lauren, and Lacey arrive early to help decorate the house with Rod decorations, and they all agree with Belle and AJ that it was an absolute waste of money.

'Oh God,' I say, attaching the banner to the wall as Sabrina holds the chair I am standing on. I recently noticed that the Faces posters I ordered did not arrive on time. Do you think anyone would mind?

'No,' she sighed. 'No one will care about any of this except you.'

The first visitors to arrive at seven o'clock on the dot are my charming, very boisterous new American friend, whom I have only met once before, and her bearded boyfriend. It's evident they've been drinking all day. They've also brought their Cavalier King Charles Spaniel, adorned in a small Christmas jumper.

The other guests don't arrive until nine o'clock, so we try to catch up with our first two, but, alas, the boyfriend drops out on the sofa with his spaniel on top of him for the rest of the evening, putting him in plain sight of everybody entering the party. Friends arrive slowly, one by one. Things are stilted. The man remains passed out with the dog on him, creating an eye-catching sight upon entering the gathering. One attendee - a friend of a friend, a music video director from the hip Peckham contingent - walks in, takes one look at the tableau, pretends he has another event to attend that he forgot about, and leaves.

Halfway through the evening, I go to the bathroom to get away from the throng, which is made up of completely different social groupings who have nothing to say to each other, with 'You Wear It Well' playing on repeat in the background while people gripe about the Rod-only playlist. AJ and Belle are in there, AJ on the toilet and Belle on the side of the bathtub. We discuss how horrible the party is. We brainstorm strategies to convince people to leave and bring the situation to a conclusion. AJ says she has to lie down for ten minutes since she is exhausted and miserable. There is a knock on the restroom door, and my brother enters.

'Quite a bizarre crowd down there, fellas,' he remarks.

When I return downstairs, the guest mass has shrunk even further. A very tall skinhead bloke in a leather bomber jacket raids the refrigerator.

'Um. Hi. Who are you? I inquire.

'I was advised to come here,' the man replies with a heavy Romanian accent, drinking from a can of beer he's helped himself to. 'For delivery.'

'Delivery?'

'Yes,' he answers, staring at me conspiratorially. 'Delivery.'

'OK, would you mind just--' I lead him to the front door, 'just waiting here.' I pass by the American, who is slow-dancing with her be-jumpered dog to 'Sailing' in front of a puzzled audience. Her lover has been passed out on the sofa for more than three hours.

'RIGHT, I THINK SOMEONE'S DRUG DEALER IS HERE,' I

announce angrily to the audience. 'I'm sorry to be a party pooper, and I don't blame you for wanting to get high at this dreadful party, but could you maybe ask all of your drug sellers to wait outside or in the hallway?'

The party ends just after midnight.

The next morning over coffee, Belle and I conduct a two-man Chilcot Inquiry into how everything went so wrong. I believe that my preparation for the theme may have set unrealistic expectations.

'You built a rod for your own back,' she says, nodding wisely.

We keep Rod Stewart's cardboard cutout in the living room for a while. A caution not to get ahead of oneself in this life. We dress him up thematically, putting on a pink bra during the Lord Sewel hooker controversy and a leprechaun's cap for St. Patrick's Day. When we move out eight months later and pack up the house, we leave nothing but the Rod Stewart cut-out in the middle of the living room, passing on the curse of bad parties to the next renters.

THE BAD DATE DIARIES: A MID-MORNING, COMPLETELY SOBER SNOG

Spring 2014. On a Saturday morning, I wake up to my alarm at nine a.m. after only five hours of sleep. There is a WhatsApp message from dishy American Martin saying, 'Doll face - we still on for a cup of joe?' My skull feels like it's been turned inside out like a dirty sock, but I assure him I'll be there. We met on Tinder three days ago, and it's been a steady stream of 'No way that's my favourite Springsteen album!', 'I believe in reincarnation too', 'Yes, perhaps we are all wanderers', and so on. As I search my room for last night's fake eyelashes and glue them back on, I am confident he will be my boyfriend by the end of the week, and we will move to Seattle together next month. For a single, hungover woman who is ashamed about falling off a bus the night before, marriage and deportation are the only sensible options.

The costume consists of an enormous Aran jumper that hangs like a dress, denim hot pants because all of my jeans are dirty, laddered tights, and white plimsolls.

'No coat?' my hungover flatmate AJ asks as I speed by her on the stairs. 'No need,' I reply breezily.

'You STINK of Baileys, by the way,' she exclaims as I shut the door.

Martin is seated at the bar of Caravan King's Cross. Fortunately, he is exactly to his images. He's writing in a notebook when I arrive, which I believe adds a great touch of theatrical to the wandering lost-soul agenda he promotes on his quirky Instagram account, which I've already stalked.

'What are you writing?' I inquire over his shoulder. He turns, looks at me, and smiles.

'None of your business,' he responds, kissing me on both cheeks. It's already very flirtatious, and we haven't even had coffee, let alone six drinks. I guess it's because he's American.

Martin informs me about his life: An illustrator from Seattle, reaching forty, earned a lot of money from a huge assignment and chose to spend it to tour the world for a year while writing a book. To meet new people, he is engaging in 'Tinder tourism'. He's been in England for a month and plans to spend a few more weeks in London before continuing his travels.

(Aside: I noticed at the time that Martin was particularly vague when I asked him what his book was about, other than saying it was non-fiction. I also noticed he wrote a couple of things down when I was talking. He took the notebook with him when he went to the loo and was in there for quite a long time. I decided either A) his bowels had a bad reaction to caffeine and he wanted to pass some time on the loo relaxing with his thoughts; B) he was just a private man and sensed I was a nosey, hung-over person with no boundaries who might want to read his notebook when he went to the loo; C) he was writing something embarrassing like his cosmic shopping list or how many people he had slept with and didn't want me to read it; or D) he was writing a book about all the women he'd dated in England and I was up next. I have always thought it was option D and to this day am still waiting to see a book called Green and Pleasant Slags: My Time With English Women on the shelves at Waterstones with an embarrassing paragraph about me in it.)

After our coffees, we sit on a seat outside the cafe, starring at the water fountains that shoot in a rhythmic, sexual manner, and he cites Hemingway, which I think is a little excessive, but I'm enjoying the imaginative tone of the date, so I go with it. He takes out another notebook, which he has filled with maps of every place he has visited thus far, as well as sketches of his tracks in the form of tiny footprints.

I inquire if he has a girl in each port. He smiles and says'something like that' in his obnoxious but charming accent.

He takes my hand and guides me down the steps in front of Central Saint Martins Art College to the canal. We walk for a little distance till we arrive at the nearest bridge, at which point he unbuttons his coat, pulls me in, and wraps it over me. He kisses my forehead, cheeks, neck, and lips. We kissed for a half hour.

The time is 11 a.m.

Martin and I parted ways at 11:30 a.m. and thanked each other for a nice morning. I'm back in bed by 12:30 and sleep all afternoon. I wake up at four a.m., thinking that I had imagined the entire affair.

Predictably, Martin disappears after our coffee morning and is cryptic about our next date when he does contact us. A week later, fueled by Friday-night Prosecco and encouraged by my friends, I send Martin a WhatsApp message littered with spelling errors, asking if I'may be frank' and suggesting we go on a 'platonic but sexual relationship' while he is in London. I advise that I become his 'girl at the London port'. I say it's 'what Hemingway would do'.

Martin never messaged me again.

EVERYTHING I KNEW ABOUT LOVE AT TWENTY-FIVE

Men adore a lady who suppresses her emotions. Make them wait five dates, or at least three, before having sex with you. This is how you keep people interested.

Your best friends' boyfriends will stick around, which is annoying. Most of them will not be the person you expected your best buddy to wind up with.

Suspenders and stockings can be purchased inexpensively and in bulk on eBay.

Online dating is for losers, and I include myself. Be extremely wary of anyone who pays to have an embarrassing profile on a dating site.

Forget what I mentioned previously about utilizing hair removal cream when dating someone. If you go bald, you're disappointing the sisterhood. We must aggressively resist patriarchal control over female anatomy.

Never make an album as amazing as Blood on the Tracks 'our record' with a boyfriend because you will be unable to listen to it years later. Don't make that mistake at 21.

If a man loves you because you are slim, he is not a real man.

If you think you want to break up with someone but practical issues are standing in the way, here's a test: imagine you could walk into a room and click a large red button that would end your relationship without a hassle. There will be no breakup conversations, no tears, and no gathering up your belongings from his residence. Would you do it? If the answer is yes, you must break up with them.

If a man has always been single at the age of 45, there is a reason. Do not wait around to find out what it is.

The worst feeling in the world is being dumped because they say they don't like you anymore.

Always invite a man back to your home, where you can deceive him into staying for breakfast and falling in love with you.

Casual sex is rarely satisfying.

Fake orgasms make you feel guilty and miserable, and they are unjust to the guy. Use them sparingly.

Some ladies get lucky, while others don't. There are both nice and terrible guys. It's pure luck who you wind up with and how you're treated.

Your best pals will leave you for males. It will be a long and slow goodbye, but accept it and create new acquaintances.

On long, lonely nights when your concerns crawl over your head like bugs and you can't sleep, imagine being loved in another lifetime, one of toil and blood. Remember how it felt to be sheltered in someone's arms. Hope you locate it again.

REASONS TO HAVE A BOYFRIEND AND REASONS NOT TO HAVE A BOYFRIEND

Reasons to having a boyfriend: - More likely to receive a proper birthday cake. Access to Sky TV?

- Find something to chat about on Sunday afternoons. More sympathy when you do something seriously wrong at work - Someone to grope your bottom in the wait for popcorn— Holidays for one are extremely pricey. And it's impossible to apply sunscreen on your own back. Sometimes you can't manage a full huge pizza by yourself. Possible ownership of a vehicle. It's nice to cook a sandwich for someone other than yourself. It's also nice to consider someone other than yourself. Regular, non-atypical sexual activity. Warmer bed: Everyone else has one. If you have one, people will believe you are lovable. If you don't have one, people will assume you are shallow and disordered. - The relief of not having to flirt with people- Fear of dying alone, emptiness, etc.

Reasons Not to Have a Boyfriend: Everyone annoys you except you - "Debates" - They probably won't like Morrissey, and they certainly won't like Joni Mitchell. They'll point out when you tell exaggerated stories. - Going to their buddies' dull birthday drinks in Finsbury Park - Being told what you did the night before while inebriated - Sharing pudding - Watching live or televised sports - Having to spend time with their friends' women and discuss The Voice. Constantly traipsing around between flats with knickers in your bag. Being open about your emotions - Having to keep your room really neat and tidy. Not reading as much. Having to keep your phone fully charged at all times so he knows you're not dead. You'll probably miss flirting with folks. Hairs are all over the bathroom.

TOTTENHAM COURT ROAD AND ORDERING SHIT OFF AMAZON

When I was twenty-one, nearing the end of my final summer performing at the Edinburgh Festival before returning home to find a job and begin my adult life, I went out to celebrate my friend Hannah's thirtieth birthday. She had been directing me in a comedic sketch production for which I had been flyering, and to celebrate, two of the other performers and I brought her to a luxury restaurant. She had made some vague comments about dreading turning thirty in the days leading up to the day, which we all felt were overdone for comedic effect.

Halfway through supper, she set down her silverware and began crying.

'Oh my God, Hannah, are you that upset?I asked, instantly regretting the 'Happy Birthday Granny' card I had handed her.

'I am getting older,' she added. I can feel it. I can feel it throughout my body, and it's already slowing down. And it will just get slower.'

'You're still so young!Margaret, who was a few years older than her, said, but Hannah continued to sob, unable to catch her breath, tears dropping into her plate. Do you want to go?' she inquired, stroking Hannah's back. Hannah nodded.

We were walking down Princes Street, chatting about nothing, hoping to keep the tone light and Hannah distracted, when she stopped in the middle of the road and clutched her head in her hands. Her tears turned into wails.

Is this it?"She asked, shouting into the black night. Is this really all there is to life?'

Is this what all life is?' Margaret inquired soothingly, wrapping her arm around her.

She replied, "Fucking Tottenham Court Road and ordering shit from Amazon."

For years, those words remained stuck on the underside of my mind, like a Post-it note I couldn't get off. They hung there like a whispered discussion between your parents that you couldn't comprehend but knew was very important. I've often puzzled why those two things, Tottenham Court Road and Amazon, could bring so much grief.

'You'll understand when you're not twenty-one,' Hannah replied when I inquired.

I finally understood the intricacies and subtext of that term the year I turned twenty-five. When you start to wonder if life is truly simply waiting for buses on Tottenham Court Road and ordering books you'll never read from Amazon, you are experiencing an existential crisis. You're realizing how mundane life is. You're finally realizing how little there is to anything. You're transitioning from the realm of fiction 'when I grow up' to the reality that you're present; it's occurring. And it was not what you expected. You aren't who you expected to be.

Once you start digging a hole full with those questions, it's tough to take the day-to-day functions of life seriously. Throughout my twenty-fifth year, it was as if I had dug a trench of my own thoughts and unanswerable questions, and from the darkness, I peered up, watching people care about the same things I had cared about: haircuts, the newspaper, parties, dinner, January sales on Tottenham Court Road, Amazon deals - and I couldn't imagine climbing out and knowing how to immerse myself in any of it again.

I took up drinking for a while to attempt to balance my mood, but it only made me overthink even more. I attempted Tinder dating, but the mostly platonic interactions left me feeling depressed and empty. My once-passionate love and dedication for my profession was waning. My flatmates, AJ and Belle, frequently entered my room to find me crying while still wrapped in a towel from a shower I had taken three hours earlier. I couldn't express how I felt to anyone, so I spent a lot of time alone. My body hummed with apathy, ennui, and worry, as low and disturbing as a washing machine on a spin cycle that wouldn't stop. All of this culminated in the early summer, when Dilly told me she felt I should quit my job to become a full-time writer, leaving me with no idea how to make money or where to go next. AJ also stated that she was going out to live with her partner, less than a year after Farly had left. I was sad, unemployed, and without a housemate.

The response, of course, was the same as it always is for a single twenty-something lady prone to melodrama: relocate to another city. I had always loved New York and would frequently see Alex, who remained a close friend even after her brother Harry ended our connection years before. In the summer of my dissatisfaction, she got engaged and asked me to be her bridesmaid, which felt opportune. She and her fiancé invited Farly and I to stay in their Lower East Side apartment for free while they were on honeymoon. We reserved flights, a hotel for the wedding, and a one-night trip to the Catskill Mountains near the conclusion of our two-week stay. Unbelievably, this would be Farly and my first trip abroad together. And it was an excellent opportunity for me to assess my potential new home: its daily operations, its personnel, and how I could picture myself fitting in.

However, Florence was diagnosed with leukemia just a week before our flight. Farly naturally felt compelled to stay at home to help her sister and family. I asked whether she needed me there too, but she urged me to travel to New York on my own and have a much-needed break.

In my first two days in New York, I was caught up in a fun hurricane of bridesmaid duties. Alex's whole British contingent had flown in for the wedding, and the preparations included crafting wreaths, arranging chairs, picking up items from the dry cleaners, and catching up with old and familiar acquaintances. I missed Farly badly, yet I still craved the bustling, new, and beautiful embrace of distraction.

On the wedding day, I wore a black strappy dress with a thigh-high split (Alex encouraged this because she knew I needed a holiday romance; I also knew I'd be seeing Harry for the first time in years), and I read the poem 'The Amorous Shepherd' in the Brooklyn warehouse where they married. I couldn't help but cry when I spoke the sentence, 'I don't regret anything I was before since I still am; I only regret not having loved you. For Alex and her husband's love for one other, and for the loneliness I had only recently understood I had experienced over the previous year.

I was one of two single women at the wedding, and I considered myself fortunate to have been seated next to the only single male guest: a big Welshman who constructed bridges for a job.

'Good poem,' he remarked to me in his seductive, seesawing, sing-songy voice. 'The tears were a lovely touch.'

'It was not planned!I said.

'That dress surely was,' he added with a smile.

We drank Negroni after Negroni, ate fried chicken and mac and cheese, and flirted in ways that are only appropriate when you're the only two single people at a wedding. We conducted a thorough review of all of our top bridges in Britain. I gave him pudding off my fork. He cheered for me when I stood up to deliver my speech and winked when I caught his eye halfway through. He acted like he had been my boyfriend for many years. Our connection grew in familiarity like a foot on a pedal pressed right to the floor (in a way that is only appropriate when you are the only two single people at a wedding).

My Welshman disappeared just before the first dance to answer a phone call outside. Alex escorted her husband to the dance floor, wearing a rose crown and a long, white, kimono-sleeved dress that made her look like a silk-draped Pre-Raphaelite. The humming undulation of the most beautiful music I'd ever heard played - Phil Phillips' 'Sea Of Love' - was the ultimate slow dance.

By the chorus, all of the other guests had joined in, with tens of couples, including Harry and his new girlfriend, swaying and smiling to the sweetly romantic song. I sat on the outside, peering within. I attempted to fathom what it would be like to feel secure in the person you go to bed with, which was a completely foreign concept to me. I pictured the spaces between their bodies; the stories they had written together; the memories, language, habits, trust, and future dreams they would have talked while drinking wine late at night on the sofa. I pondered if I could ever have it with someone, or if I was even meant to float in a sea of love. If I even wanted to. I felt a tap on my shoulder and turned up to see Octavia, another bridesmaid. She smiled and extended her hand to lead me to the dance floor, where we danced until the song ended.

After that, I drank the Negronis even harder. When I stepped outside for a cigarette and spotted my Welshman, Campari gave me the confidence to press him against the brick wall and kiss him.

'I can't do that,' he murmured, backing away.

Why not?' I asked.

'It doesn't matter,' he mumbled. 'But I simply cannot.'

'No,' I muttered. 'This is not happening like this. I'm in New York, on vacation, a melancholy bridesmaid, and I'm wearing a slaggy dress with a split that I paid to have taken up even higher at the dry cleaners. You're my holiday fling, OK? It has been decided.

'I can't' he replied. 'I would like to, but I can't.'

'So, what was with all the -' I mimed putting pudding in his mouth. 'And the--' I gave an overdone, theatrical wink.

'I was only flirting,' he admitted faintly.

Yeah, that was a complete waste of time. Did you know I was seated next to a very intriguing and clever actor? I would have loved to talk to her. She appeared fascinating. I guess I said maybe three words to her entire night. I was too busy pretending to be your girlfriend.'

'Oh well, I'm sorry I wasted your time!He huffed and walked back into the party.

The next day, I went to Alex and her new husband's flat in Chinatown to bid them farewell on their honeymoon and toast their new marriage from the roof. We caught up on wedding rumors, and they explained the Welshman's confused signals (he had a girlfriend, of course).

Alex gave me a tour of the apartment and handed over the keys.

Are you going to be okay?' she inquired.

'I'll be alright,' I responded.

'Have you got Octavia's number? She is in the city till the end of the month, so you are not alone.

I'll be alright; it's healthy for me to spend some time alone. Get to know New York better. It will be a fantastic adventure.'

She hugged me and added, "You call us if you need anything."

I absolutely will not. 'Go to Mexico, bathe naked in the water, drink tequila, and shag yourself into oblivion,' I advised.

The next morning, I awoke in the apartment, fed their two black cats, watered their plants as directed, and sat with a notepad to plan how I was going to spend my time here and what I would see and do.

But there was one major problem: a magazine was late paying me for two pieces of work totaling just under a thousand pounds, which I had anticipated to be more than enough for my New York expenses. I had £34 in my account and eleven days remaining in New York. As a freelance journalist, I was frequently chasing accounts departments for money three months after a story had been published and the invoice filed. But it had never been so urgent. I called my editor; my editor forwarded me to the accounts department; and that department passed me from person to person, attempting to figure out where my late payment was. I lay on Alex's bed for an hour with my phone on loudspeaker, the tinny hold music blaring and the long-distance phone call adding to my bill minute by minute. The guy I spoke with concluded that I will be paid 'soon'.

With no money and no friends, it was clear that New York was not the same as the previous times I had visited Alex on vacation. It's not a pleasant place to be broke. Unlike London, all museums and galleries require a general admission fee, usually $25, which would have depleted my remaining finances. It was also the middle of August, so the heat was unbearable, limiting the amount of time I could spend wandering around or sitting in the park. The city I had always loved, where I had always felt welcome, seemed to want me to leave. When I walked along Fifth Avenue, the towers seemed like big, terrible, towering creatures chasing me to JFK Airport.

I started to notice all the little things I despised about New York that hadn't troubled me before. I noticed how inefficient and complex the metro was. Unlike the London Underground, which has a colorful and sometimes regal assortment of line names (Jubilee, Victoria, Piccadilly), the lines have all been given the most indistinguishable and lackluster names possible (A, B, C, 1, 2, 3, etc.). And B can easily sound like D, and 1 could possibly be 3. It is impossible to remember which letter or number you are supposed to catch without writing it down. Trains only come every 10 minutes at many stations, so if you're making three changes and luck isn't on your side, you could be standing around for an extra half-hour on boiling hot platforms. To make matters worse, the majority of platforms lack any signage indicating when the next train is scheduled to arrive.

Then there were the New York 'ball-busters', the loud, demanding folks in shops, cafes, and lines who snapped at you. The ones that are either extremely unpleasant or trying to provide you with 'the whole immersive New York experience'. Perhaps I found it hilarious because I was feeling secure and cheerful. But now, feeling so alone, I despised how much I was shouted at. "HEY, LADY, GET OUT OF THE FRIKKIN' WAY!'" A passing waiter barked at me in Katz's Deli as I stood at the counter ordering a bagel.

I also observed how often I was shoved in New York. The combined ambition of the place has never felt so daunting. Everyone was focused on their own objective, and no one looked at each other. People power-walked, flailing their arms like they were marching and shouted into their hands-free devices. Even their romance was ambitious; I spent an entire afternoon eavesdropping on two female friends at a cafe talking about how they were going to meet guys, and they made it sound like a military operation, complete with dates, figures, arithmetic, and rules.

And, Christ, the regulations. I had never realized how preoccupied they all were with rules. I got told off for picking up and smelling an orange at the supermarket before purchasing it. When I went to Apthorp (Nora Ephron's favorite apartment complex, on which she wrote an essay), I was told off for getting too close to the beautiful fountain in the courtyard. I had never considered myself to be particularly anarchic, but the disciplinarians of New York brought it out in me.

Then there were the unfunny hipsters. People who gave you fine coffee or worked in cool stores; those who plainly replied, 'That's the funniest thing I've ever heard in my whole life,' with a straight, expressionless face when someone told them a joke, rather than laughing. The ones that stared at you for longer than they felt comfortable doing. There is no self-awareness, humour, or cynicism; only the mentality of a Hackney twat. Scenesters under the age of thirty in New York are among the coldest and most uninviting persons I've ever encountered.

A week into my huge New York vacation, I discovered that places are kingdoms of memories and relationships, and that the environment is always a reflection of how you feel inside. I felt more empty, exhausted, and depressed there than I did at home. The fantasy of moving vanished with each passing day. I had the unsettling realization that 'Tottenham Court Road and Amazon' would accompany me wherever I went; I was still the same unfulfilled person on vacation as I was at home. When I booked the flights, I assumed I was planning a trip in my thoughts, but I wasn't. The external scenery had changed, but the inside things remained the same: I felt worried, restless, and self-loathing.

One night, as I lay on Alex's sofa, drinking a bottle of leftover wedding Prosecco that she had told me to help myself to, I spent the evening trying 'Tinder tourism' to meet new people. I right-swiped almost everyone. I sent a vague, cheerful broadcast message to all of my matches, introducing myself as a 'visitor from London' searching for some New Yorkers to'show her a good time'. At midnight, I opened a second bottle of Prosecco, just in time to take a video call from AJ and India.

'Heeeeeeeey!They shouted together from around my kitchen table.

Hello, guys!I said. 'Are you pissed?'

'Yes,' India replied. 'We just went to Nisa Local and purchased three bottles of wine.

'Good. I'm also pissed.

Who are you with?AJ inquired, staring into the webcam. I considered telling them what a dreadful time I was having, but I did not want to worry them. And, more crucially, my pride would not permit it. I had been persuading everyone on social media that I was having the trip of a lifetime.

'No one,' I responded. 'I'm having some downtime tonight.'

We caught up for fifteen minutes, and I was glad to see their familiar faces and hear everything about their activities.

'Are you okay?AJ inquired when I said goodbye. 'You seem down.'

'I'm OK,' I replied. I miss you both.

'We miss you, too!' she stated. They both blew kisses at me before leaving me alone again.

Halfway through my second bottle of Prosecco, I received a message from one of my Tinder matches, Jean, an attractive thirty-two-year-old French stockbroker, who asked if I wanted a late drink. I determined that this man would be my holiday fling; just the kind of wonderful, empowering experience I needed to transform this trip into an adventure and make me feel like myself again. But he lived in

SoHo, a mile away, which I couldn't walk because there was a thunderstorm outside, and I didn't have enough money in my account to pay for a taxi.

'I have money,' he wrote. 'I'll pay for your taxi.' I decided to disregard the Pretty Woman subtext of this offer, put on some mascara and heels, and waited in the rain for a passing cab. As I hailed one, a combination of torrential rain and torrential alcohol caused my phone to slide from my grasp. The screen shattered into a hundred bits, raindrops leaked into the cracks, and the image faded to black.

When I got to the address he gave me, he was, thankfully, standing outside. He paid for the cab and opened the door so I could get out.

'Thanks for coming,' he said, bringing my face to his for a kiss. For a brief while, the attention of this perfect stranger filled me with a light fizz of exhilaration, and the gravity of my deep-seated despair felt as if it had left the premises. Then I realized how pathetic and telling this was, and I was instantly sadder. I needed another beverage.

Jean seemed nice enough. We had nothing in common, but conversation flowed thanks to the beer he offered me and the Lucky Strike packet we smoked on his sofa. I got the impression he did this a lot. After an hour of talking and snogging, he led me to his bedroom. A stark white box with unusual neon lights and a mattress on the floor instead of a bed. I tried to ignore the setting while we undressed each other.

'Wait, wait,' he said as I undid his jeans. 'I only do group sex.'

'What? What does that mean? I slurred.

'I can only have sex if someone watches,' he said as if it were simple logic. 'Or if somebody joins us.'

'OK,' I replied. 'Well, that's not going to happen now, so—'

'My flatmate is next door,' he explained. 'He wants to come inside. "I'll tell him it's okay?"

'No, it's not okay,' I responded, suddenly realizing that this was not a huge adventure at all. I was in a bedroom with a man who could have been Patrick Bateman. 'I don't want to do that,' I murmured, scared, my heart racing in my ears and looked for the nearest window.

'Come on, it'll be wonderful,' he urged, attempting to kiss me. 'You looked like a party girl.'

'No, I am not; I do not want to do that.'

'Okay, we don't do that.' He shrugged and rolled over.

I understood how silly this was, how irresponsible I had been in my pursuit for an escape from myself. I was alone in an unfamiliar city, inebriated; no one knew where I was; and I had no money or a phone.

'I suppose I'm going to walk home,' I remarked, getting out of bed.

'OK,' he responded. 'It is raining, though. You can stay here if you want.

I looked at his clock: four a.m. I could sleep until the storm passed and it was light out, then try to find my way back to Alex's flat. I fell asleep as far away from him as I could, with my face crushed against his white wall.

The next morning, I awoke at half past seven, dressed, and walked into the living room to get my suitcase. A man in a navy dressing robe sat on the sofa, appearing really upset. Four electric fans appeared that had not been present the night before, and all of the windows were open. There were pieces of paper affixed to the wall, each with FUMER TUE scrawled in red pen and SMOKING KILLS written underneath.

'Good morning!' I replied anxiously.

'Get. Ze ferk. 'Get out of my place,' he said with a thicker French accent than Jean's.

'I am sorry?'

'I've got asthma. Do you know that? I have severe asthma. So, why are you at my apartment at three in the morning, chain-smoking your awful cigarettes?

'I'm sorry; Jean said it was fi-'

'Jean can go ferk 'imself,' he spat.

I went back into Jean's bedroom.

'Hey,' I replied, shaking him awake. 'Hey, your flatmate is in there, and he's going bananas.'

Jean opened his eyes and looked at the clock.

'I'm late for work!' he exclaimed accusatorily.

'He's getting pretty frantic in there,' I added. 'He's unhappy because we smoked last night. He has all these supporters and has written all these signs. It feels a little... Rain Man.

'He is not angry because we were smoking; he is angry because you refused to have sex with him.'

'Okay, I'm going,' I said. Have a good life. I stepped out of the flat, shyly nodding at my enraged French housemate as I departed.

'Get out. GET OUT. 'GET ZE FERK OUT, YOU LITTLE BEETCH!' he exclaimed after me.

I teetered into the bright SoHo sunshine, feeling like I was about to retch. I attempted to withdraw ten dollars from the nearest ATM but was told I did not have enough funds. A wave of illness swept through me, and I realized I hadn't eaten in two days.

As I attempted to find my way home, I entered Starbucks, hoping that they had left jugs of milk among the sugar sachets. I asked the man behind the counter for a paper cup and filled it with milk, which I sipped carefully while sitting at a table.

'Are you okay, honey?' a middle-aged woman said. 'You resemble a...' She examined my clothes, my eyes ringed with last night's mascara dust, and the cup of milk in my hand. 'Like a stray kitten.'

'I am fine,' I said. I'm feeling worse than I've ever felt.

I walked around in circles for a few hours until I spotted a block of apartments I remembered. I entered Alex's apartment, buried my phone in rice, and curled up beneath her blanket with her cats, yearning to pull the duvet up for the trip as well. But I couldn't afford a sandwich, much less an early flight home. And I don't believe I really wanted to go home; I was stuck between two cities I didn't want to be in. I couldn't call Farly and ask for assistance because she needed my support far more than I did. I couldn't call my parents since I didn't want to bother them, and I was 10 years too old to be bailed out of anything. I eventually called Octavia, who treated me with incredible kindness. She took me out to dim sum, held my hand while I spoke, hugged me, and lent me some money.

The next day, I took a three-hour coach ride to a little village in the Catskills of upstate New York. Farly and I had already paid for the cabin, so I figured I might as well utilize it, and I appreciated the opportunity for some space, quiet, and open skies.

I arrived mid-morning, dropped down my stuff, and went for a lengthy stroll to clear my mind. By the time I got back to my cabin in the afternoon, after marveling at the vastness of the mountains and considering the notion of starting over when I got home, I was already feeling calmer.

In the evening, I walked into town and ate cheese fries at a nearby diner. I enjoyed the sound of crickets and the warmth and chit-chat of the people. When I went back, there was a bonfire burning behind my cabin, so I grabbed one of the blankets from my room and sat next to it, gazing at the stars. For what seemed like the first time since arriving in New York, I breathed.

When I returned to my room, I discovered a fresh Tinder message - a late response to the 'come one, come all' blanket message I had drunkenly written two nights prior. His name was Adam. He was twenty-six and had a gorgeous, all-American smile, complete with a Brooklyn beard and man bun.

'Hello, woman,' he texted. 'I apologize for not responding to this sooner; how are you?'

'I wish you had responded sooner,' I remarked. 'I could have gone on a date with you instead of being forced into a threesome with two Frenchmen.'

'Oh boy!' he wrote. "New York can be challenging. How're you doing?

'I hate it,' I responded. 'I'm in the Catskills for the night, and it's a pleasant break.'

'How long have you been back in the city before returning home?

'Three long days. I return early tomorrow evening.

'Come hang out with me when you get back,' he added. I will not try to have a threesome with you, I promise. I'll just be your friend if you want.

A friend. Perhaps I needed a new pal.

The next day, after another lengthy hike and swim, I caught a late-afternoon bus back to Manhattan, rode the subway to Brooklyn, and arrived at Adam's doorway.

'Hey,' he said, stepping from the front door, his blue eyes glittering behind horn-rimmed glasses, and reaching out his arms for a hug. 'It's great to meet you. Welcome return to the city you despise.'

'Thanks,' I replied, slipping into his embrace and enjoying the fresh, soapy scent of his flannel shirt.

I'll make you adore it.

Adam showed me around his place, and we opened a bottle of wine. We talked for hours, sharing stories about our favorite music, films, friends and family, and careers. He was eager, bright-eyed, bushy-tailed, and curious—exactly what I needed.

By mid-evening, we had kissed. By midnight, I was laying in his bed, my face close to his. It was this man's gentle touch, giving heart, and tenderness that compelled me to open myself. So I told him everything and gave it all up for free. I told him about the heartbreak of my early twenties. I told him about the years I spent starving myself in an attempt to regain control. I told him about the one time I fell in love and the intimacy I couldn't bear, as well as the reliance I was afraid of.

I told him how, one by one, my pals fell in love and abandoned me. I told him how my anxiety had creeped up on me in catatonic flare-ups since I was a child, and how I couldn't stand near windows because I was always afraid I'd fall and die. I told him about my best friend's younger sister, whom I had grown up with, who was in a hospital bed with cancer. I told him that I felt overwhelmed by maturity and that I was unable to call anyone for aid. I told him about how easily I buried difficulties in a tangled web of distractions. I only possessed the correct words to express my anguish to a stranger; I could only tell these stories in a fleeting realm of imagination where I had no accountability.

'You're so sad,' he whispered, touching my cheek. I closed my eyes to stop the tears.

'I'm really lost,' I responded.

'You're not lost anymore,' he whispered, pulling me closer to him. And for that moment, I believed him.

'I want to say something but it doesn't make sense,' he whispered, kissing my forehead.

'What?'

"I love you," he sighed. 'And I don't want you to think I'm dangerous or crazy like that insane French guy, which I know I can't be, because I've known you for -' he looked at his watch -'six hours. But I think I could love you. Fuck it; I already love you.

I heard myself respond, "I love you, too." I realized how stupid the words were the moment they came out of my mouth. But I knew I wasn't saying them to him, but to something else. To the belief in hope and love.

Adam took the next day off from work, his first sick day ever, and showed me around parts of the city I'd never been to before. We walked, spoke, ate, drank, and kissed. We had a classic holiday romance in two days; we couldn't remember what life was like without each other, but we knew we'd never be together. I stayed with him the next night.

The next day, I tore myself away from Adam for three hours to meet Octavia, who couldn't believe what had happened since our last meeting. We climbed to the top of 30 Rock and gazed out at the breathtaking, merciless city.

"I think I want to go home," I remarked, looking out at the lights dancing off the Hudson River.

Adam drove me to JFK on my final day. After a long goodbye kiss, he grabbed my shoulders and stared at me.

'Okay, I have an idea,' he said.

'What?'

"Don't think I'm nuts."

'OK.'

"Stay," he said.

'I cannot remain.'

Why not? You are miserable at home. You despise London. You do not have a job. You're not sure what you want to do next. Stay here and start again.

'Where would I live?' I inquired.

'With me,' he replied.

'How will I pay rent?'

'We'll work it out,' he explained. 'You'll be able to find job and write everything you've always wanted to write. I will offer you your own space and time. Think about how much more free you'll feel here.

'What if your ironclad immigration system tries to send me home?'

'Then I will fucking marry you,' he declared. Is this what you want to hear? Because I will do it. I'll take you to City Hall first thing tomorrow morning and marry the heck out of you. "And then you can stay as long as you want."

'I can't do that,' I replied. 'That's utterly absurd.'

'Why don't you stay?" he asked, gently leaning his head against mine. 'You were the one who stated there was nothing waiting for you at home.'

I thought for a while.

'Because I am the problem,' I responded. Not the city. None of the circumstances are the problem. I am the thing that needs to be changed. There was silence between us. And then we kissed for the final time.

'Call me when you land,' he instructed. 'And don't drink during the flight; the plane won't crash.'

On the journey home, I daydreamed about Tottenham Court Road and ordered crap from Amazon. I remembered Farly's giggle, the sound of my flatmates getting ready for work in the morning, and the scent of my mother's perfume in her hair as I hugged her. I reflected on the pleasant mundanity of existence, and how fortunate I was to be alive. The day before my twenty-sixth birthday. Belle and AJ were at work when I arrived home, but there was a weird homemade cake and a banner wishing me a happy birthday. The next evening, we all went dancing in Camden to celebrate, and I told them about my weird two-week absence. Lauren and I sat up drinking and playing guitar until the early hours of the next morning, when Adam delivered a large bouquet of red roses.

Things improved temporarily after I returned home. The thick covering of grief I'd been carrying for so long began to lift. I devised a proper plan for what I intended to accomplish next. I fell madly back in love with my city. I read Bill Bryson's books about England and ate Toffee Crisps. I reflected on how fortunate I was to live in a place where I had grown up, surrounded by friends.

Two months after my return, I quit my job and went freelancing. A month later, I was assigned a column in The Sunday Times. Lauren and I created a short film about a directionless twenty-five-year-old who has no idea who she is and turns to anything other than herself to solve the situation. AJ left, and one of our other smart university buddies, India, moved in. We left Camden's old yellow palace and relocated two miles north to a flat with no mice, a working toilet, and central heating.

Octavia, my saviour, returned to London and became a dear friend. Adam and I have always maintained in touch, and we will continue to do so; he sees me whenever he visits London, and I always have lunch with him when I visit New York. He reminds me of a turbulent period in my life, experiences that I enjoy recalling but would never want to relive. When I was twenty-five years old and feeling lost, I almost moved across the nation for a man I didn't know. He has his side of the story, and I have mine; we wear them about like cheesy teenage necklaces of a divided heart.

FLORENCE

Florence was six years old when we met, and I was barely a teenager. Farly opened the front door to see her younger sister standing on the step, swaying from side to side, her hair cropped into a tufty mop on her small head.

'FLORENCE!' she exclaimed. 'What did you do to your hair?!'

Florence smiled cheekily.

'Dad, I can't believe you let her to do this!' Farly shouted in her teenage voice to her father, Richard, who was standing by the car. "SHE LOOKS LIKE A LITTLE BOY!" Florence kept grinning.

Richard shrugged and added, "She begged to have it that way, angel." What might I do?

I adored her immediately.

Florence and I became closer as she entered adolescence. She, like me, had always felt ready to be an adult. She desired her own identity and freedom. She was weary of her peers. She escaped into literature, movies, and music. She was an obsessive, always looking for every word ever written by her new favourite writers and viewing every film ever made by her favourite directors in succession. She, like me, found it difficult to be a teenager in an all-girls school, and I constantly tried to reassure her that the best was yet to come; that being an adult, no matter how difficult or monotonous it was at times, was the best thing in the world.

'You know how people say school is the best time of your life?' I said to her one weekend afternoon as we lay in the sun in their family's yard.

'Yeah?' she replied.

'They are talking trash.'

'Really?' she murmured, rubbing my arm - it had always been a requirement for her to hang out with Farly and me when we were in our late teens.

'Yes. I've never heard so much nonsense. School days are the worst days in your life, Floss. All the good stuff only starts after you go.

'Thanks, Aldermaston,' she said (it was their family nickname for me; anybody who entered their home was given a nickname).

But Florence didn't have to worry because she matured into a terrific adolescent. Far better than I had ever been: like most teenagers, I was mostly preoccupied with myself, but Florence's worldview was broad and compassionate, especially for someone so young and having lived a rather sheltered existence. Floss was inventive, indignant, inquisitive, and passionate. She wrote a film blog, critiquing American indie filmmaking and criticizing current Hollywood. She kept daily diaries. She wrote half of a novel. She composed and directed plays that she performed at school. She spoke on LGBT concerns at her buttoned-up school assembly. She went to marches. She once came to our Camden home with a camera and two friends, asking if she might use it to shoot a short film to raise awareness about domestic violence. She also got fabulously disruptive at the dinner table. A lunch with Farly's family was almost always punctuated by Florence shrieking 'MISOGYNIST!' at someone during a heated argument. During one especially memorable dinner, she went off on Scott when he dared to criticize the artistry of Wes Anderson's films, claiming that his work was entirely aesthetic. Floss launched into a long, passionate oration, explaining why he was incorrect, before fleeing the table in a wrath and returning with a massive hardcover book about movies and slamming it on the table with a crash.

Florence was diagnosed with leukemia the summer she left school. She'd finally reached the end of youth and was on the verge of adulthood, only to be told she had cancer. However, based on what the physicians said, the outlook was optimistic, even if the treatment and recuperation would be extremely serious. And so was she, brilliantly so. She went straight to Kingston Hospital for chemotherapy and became best friends with the nurses and cleaners; she would elevate her bed as high as she could to converse with them and offer advise. She was told she wouldn't be able to have children, which many around her found sad, but she responded with uncommon elegance and good humour, claiming that the world was already overpopulated.

She established a witty, honest blog detailing her cancer journey, which attracted thousands of followers. She took selfies with her freshly shaven head and recorded humorous videos of herself dancing around her bed. She received numerous emails and messages from fans. I couldn't have been more proud of her, and I texted her frequently, telling her she had no right to be such a talented writer at the age of nineteen.

One particular post stated:

The worst thing I heard that night [on the date of her diagnosis, 8 August] wasn't actually the diagnosis but the following words: 'We want you to stay in overnight.' I didn't expect that at all. And then the doctor said, 'And in the morning the haematologist will perform a bone marrow extraction on you.' That's when I knew something was not right. They don't just DO those kind of things.

The haematologist came in to see me to say hello and introduce himself before he went home for the night. I just wanted an answer, really, so I asked him plainly, 'What do you think this is?' (gesturing to my lumpy and swollen neck). He breathed a sigh before plainly replying, '50/50 it's cancer.'

When you hear the word cancer you hear death. You think of all the prospects of your future shrivelling into non-existence. And you cry. And cry I did. This lovely man, evidently not so great with others' emotions, patted my back and attempted to comfort me with words of 'I didn't come in here to make you cry.' Well what do you expect someone to do when you tell them they've probably got cancer?! Leap in the air and yell, 'Yippee! My life just got so much better!' No, of course they're going to be upset. And I was. And I was angry. And I was worried about my parents who were crying just as much as I was.

And I remember saying, 'I'm not ready to die yet. I haven't even lived yet.' And then later on, 'And I haven't had sex yet! It's not fair.'

But I got over that stage. And now it's more like, 'When I'm done with this cancer, I'm going to kick the world in the arse and be the best thing anyone's ever seen.' I mean who can reject me, I'll have beaten cancer. Everything else is easy.

I texted her to tell her how much I enjoyed it and guaranteed her that she'd have sex once everything was finished.

'We'll go for the pull,' she said. 'I swear I'll find you a cracking fella.'

She celebrated her nineteenth birthday in the hospital, and the nurses created her a banner to hang outside her bedside. She discovered out she had been accepted to York University to study cinema, and they told her she could postpone her admission for a year until she had recovered completely. She returned home after her final cycle of chemotherapy and cooked chocolate Guinness cake for the nurses who had cared for her.

Farly's world shrunk during this period; she was either at the primary school where she now taught, in the hospital, or with her family. Scott stood by her side through it all, and I adored him for being such a steady, solid supporter of her and her family. We texted and contacted each other on a regular basis, and he would tell me how she was doing; it brought us closer together, and I felt fortunate that my closest friend had someone so strong and loving by her side.

Floss continued to blog after she returned from Kingston. Her brother, Freddie, was a bone marrow match, which was good news because it meant he could be a donor for her, however she needed to recover from chemotherapy before having the operation at a hospital in central London. However, her health quickly deteriorated, and she was admitted to the hospital prematurely. A number of problems arose in rapid succession, with none of them being resolved before the next. Her kidneys stopped working, she couldn't speak, and her organs began to fail, so she was admitted to intensive care and placed on a ventilator. Farly was allowed time off school to spend each day at the hospital with her family.

I had recently left my job of almost three years to become a full-time writer, which meant I could work from home and take the bus to meet her. We met for lunch almost every day for a month, always going to the cafe above Heal's on Tottenham Court Road and getting the same thing: two Caesar salads and a dish of chips to share. She'd tell me how Floss was doing that day, but the situation never seemed to improve. Everything was up in the air, and no one knew what would happen next; the bone marrow transplant appeared to be growing further and further away. I attempted to reassure her with the same platitudes: she's in the greatest possible situation, she's in good hands, and the doctors know what they're doing. I knew she was bombarded with statistics and facts from professionals every day, so I felt it was my responsibility as an uneducated friend to provide a positive cradle for her hope. But I had no notion what was going on.

Every day, Mom inquired about my news, hoping for some normalcy to distract and renew her before walking into the hospital room for the afternoon. I informed her of the articles I was writing that week. I showed her dudes from Tinder. She gave me a glass of Prosecco the day I found out I'd been assigned my first column, telling me she was simply delighted to celebrate something.

At one point, it appeared that Floss was making some progress, and Farly invited me to visit her in the hospital. I said I'd love to, but I was worried I wouldn't be able to hold it together. As I cleaned my hands before entering, I realized I had never visited somebody in a hospital before.

Farly said, 'Someone has come to visit you,' as I entered the room. Floss couldn't speak, but she smiled at me, and I felt comfort and a rush of love for this girl who was the closest thing I'd ever known to a younger sister. I stood at the end of her bed and babbled at her, hoping to divert her; I told her about the new Girls series, which I knew she'd adore, and about a new band I'd been listening to, which I thought she'd enjoy. Farly urged me to tell her about everything I was writing, and she smiled again when I told her about the short film Lauren and I were working on, the script of which she would have to edit for me soon. After fifteen minutes, I bid farewell to this wonderful, beautiful, electrifying thunderstorm of a girl, knowing that it might be the last time I saw her.

'I feel like I'm seeing her slip away,' Farly said me one day shortly after my visit, at one of our lunches. 'I feel it; I know it's occurring.'

'You don't know that,' I replied. 'People can go to the brink of death and then recover completely. You hear these stories all the time. But, having seen Floss so unwell and being informed that was her best day, I understood why Farly was experiencing those emotions, and it was critical that I let her to express them.

The next week, early one afternoon, I was writing at my kitchen table when Farly called.

'She is gone,' she exclaimed, panting for air. 'She has died.'

I've never seen so many people at a funeral as when we bid goodbye to Florence. All of our friends attended the ceremony, as did a large number of teachers and girls from her school, relatives, and friends she made on her travels; hundreds of individuals had been affected by her warmth, wit, brilliance, and kindness over the years. There were so many people that many had to stand outside the crematorium and watch the service on a screen. When I understood this, I smiled up at the sky, hoping it would make her happy and ensure she knew how much she was loved. Freddie delivered the eulogy, and the rabbi, who had known her since she was a child, praised her charisma and courage. Florence's best friend performed a reading of a magnificent piece she had written for her yearbook page. 'It may appear that life is difficult at times, but it is truly as simple as breathing in and out,' she wrote. 'Rip open hearts with your rage and shatter egos with your humility. Be the person you want you could be, not the one you believe you are destined to be. Allow yourself to become carried away by your emotions. You were created so that someone would adore you. Let them love you.

Between the funeral and the shiva, which is a period of mourning in the Jewish faith that occurs at home, all of the girls returned to our residence. We went to Ivan's to pick up some wine. I prepared a large pan of scrambled eggs while India cooked endless rounds of bread. We chatted about Florence, everything that was amusing, bright, and outrageous about her; we cried, laughed, and lifted our glasses in her memory.

The family residence was as full for the shiva as it had been for the funeral. We all stood in the kitchen as the rabbi said prayers and mentioned Florence. Farly began reading a poem, and I watched her say the lines into the microphone, looking smaller than I'd ever seen her. She paused at a specific sentence and began to cry, so she handed the poem to the rabbi, who continued to read it aloud. I glanced across the packed kitchen at this petite, birdlike creature, her bones and words dissolving, and I wanted to surge through the room and grab her. It was the worst moment of my life.

People stayed up late into the evening. Florence's school pals sat in her bedroom, surrounded by books and clothes. I had been assigned the condolences book. India, AJ, and Lacey were drinking Bristol Cream Sherry from plastic cups, which Aunty Laura had provided. Farly's colleagues from the school where she taught had all come to pay their respects, including the head teacher. Halfway through the evening, as is customary in Jewish culture, the bereaved family sat in a line of chairs while mourners wished them a long life.

I approached Farly and crouched down to hug her.

'I love you so much,' I said. 'I wish you a long and happy life.'

'Thank you,' she replied, squeezing my back. 'Have you seen all the teachers at my school?'

'Yes. They are wonderful. I've just spoken with your deputy head. "Do you like her?"

'I do. We had a terrific conversation; what a nice woman.

'I'm glad you like her,' she replied, smiling. 'What did you two talk about?

'I asked her to care after you when you return to work,' I explained. 'I wanted her to make sure someone was always looking after you.'

'I'll be fine, Doll,' she murmured, her large brown eyes welling up with tears till one escaped through her lashes and ran down her face. 'I just need to find a way to live without her.'

Farly and I spent the next few days in our family home together. There wasn't much chatting, but I made tea and we assisted her stepmother, Annie, with any chores around the house. After Florence died, a Telegraph journalist discovered her blog and contacted the family to ask if they may publish excerpts from it, along with an accompanying feature on her. They agreed because they knew it was what she would have wanted, and the piece prompted even more people to contact Annie and Richard to express their grief over the loss of someone so full of life.

'Send letters,' Annie urged one morning as she sat looking through a large stack of cards and letters from individuals expressing their sympathy. 'I used to be concerned that writing about something horrible happening to someone would be an invasion of privacy. It's never an imposition; it's always beneficial. If there's one thing we can take from this, it's to always just send the letter.

That afternoon, we all went for a walk with our dogs. Farly and I strolled side by side. We wore matching bobble hats that we had purchased a few days prior when we went to Kew retail park to get insoles for the shoes she wore to the burial. With the rigorous week of inseparable company, matching hats, and adults behind us, we felt like teenagers again. Except this time, we weren't talking about boys on MSN. We had stopped pretending to be grown-ups after fifteen years of walking side by side, from school to university lectures to the streets outside our first home in London.

She once told me that she did not want to be forgotten. "I feel bad about resuming normal life," she remarked.

'She said it before she realized she was dying,' I reasoned. 'I know she would have detested the idea of you mourning her forever.'

I suppose.

'You can find a method to keep her near to you and live with her without disrupting your life.

'Everything will seem strange without her.'

'It will be the new normal,' I added. 'But she made fucking sure she would not be forgotten, don't worry.'

'That's true,' she replied.

'You need to live. You do not have an option. You either move forward or plunge under.

We proceeded to walk alongside the river. It was chilly and sunny, as quiet and clear as a day in an unshaken snow globe. We strolled past a series of cottages in Chiswick with brightly coloured doors. The whitewashed pubs faced the chilly, watery breeze. Aside from the bridges with tube trains speeding by, we could have been in a seaside village.

'Ant and Dec reside down here,' she explained, nodding toward the cottages. 'In one of these.'

No, they don't.

They do, I promise.

"They don't. You're just saying that because the front doors are so small."

'I promise you, they reside here.'

'Together?'

'No, not together; they live next door to one another.'

We went on walking.

'I never want to live far away from you,' I stated.

'Me neither.'

'I don't care where I live when I grow up; all I want is to be close to you.'

'Me, too.'

'Even now, we seem too far apart. I want us to make sure our residences are really close together. I want to make it a priority from now on.

'So do I,' she replied.

We continued along the river, the December sun still shining in the sky.

I always think about you when the weather is like this. This is your favorite kind of day,' I explained.

'It is. Cold and brilliant.'

'Yes. My preference is dark and rainy because I am a self-indulgent neurotic, and you are always bouncing and buoyant.

'Ha.'

'YOU ARE. We got it wrong when we were youngsters. We always assumed you were the sensitive one, but it turns out I'm the one who is constantly a mess. You're considerably more resilient than you realize.'

'I am not sure about that,' she said.

'YOU ARE. You are made of the strongest material. I wouldn't be able to cope if this were my situation.

'You don't realize that. You never know how you're going to respond to something until it happens to you. We continued to walk beside one other, watching the sunshine shimmer off the sea. 'It has been like this every day since she died.'

'She's here,' I announced. 'She is with us. She will be there whenever you point out an injustice or giggle at your favorite movie. She'll be there.

We strolled along Kew Bridge, Annie and her sister still visible behind us, and a bruiser of a dog trotted beside them, tail swooshing from side to side.

'Would you like to be cremated?' she inquired.

'I do,' I replied. 'And I want to be distributed throughout Devon. At Mothecombe Beach.'

'Me too,' she replied. But I want to be spread where Floss will be, in Cornwall. I regret that I will not be with you.

'Oh, that's okay; we'll be together wherever we go next. We will just have to meet there.

'Definitely.'

'Do you think it's a little lonely for me to be on the beach by myself? What about Hampstead Heath? It's my favourite place in London, and my parents used to take me there as a child.

'No, definitely not; you'll get stamped on.'

'Yes, you're correct. "And too posh and predictable."'

'That's why I think it's lovely to be spread in the water,' she remarked thoughtfully. 'I am afraid of sharks.' 'But you'll be dead already.'

'Oh yes.'

'That's the whole purpose; the shark might do its worst and you'd still be alright. You've passed the point of no return.

'Okay, at sea then.'

We strolled home in the wonderful sunshine, and I was glad for Florence's life and everything that she had taught me. I was grateful for the sun on Kew Bridge as I put one foot in front of the other. I was grateful for the realization that life might be as easy as breathing in and out. And I was grateful to understand what it meant to love the person walking with me as much as I did. So deep, so fierce. It's just impossible.

MY THERAPIST SAYS

'Why are you here?'

Why was I there? I never imagined I would be there. In a modest room behind Oxford Circus, with cream carpets and a burgundy sofa. Where it always smelled like molecular perfume and nothing else, no matter how hard I inhaled when I walked in - no leftover lunch, no cooling coffee, no sign of a life outside this room other than this woman's perfume. When I caught a whiff of it on a woman at a party, it always made my heart sink and reminded me of one p.m. on a Friday afternoon. I was looking for a fee per the hour. A commentator's box, the TV studio of post-match analysis, amid a lifeless vacuum where there was only interaction between two persons. The less popular discussion show that airs alongside the main event. This was Strictly: It takes two. This was Dancing on Ice: Defrosted. This was the room I would always imagine when I was about to make a stupid decision:

in a bar lavatory, with a man in the back of a taxi. This chamber promised to improve my life.

I always promised myself that I would never be in a room like this. But I didn't know where else to be. I'd run out of other alternatives. I was twenty-seven years old, and I felt like I was about to collapse from anxiety. It had been nine months since I went freelance, and I had spent almost every day alone with my thoughts. I had ignored the concerns of my friends and family; I was constantly on the point of tears, but I couldn't talk to anyone. Every morning, I awoke with no idea where I was or what was going on; it was as if the previous night's sleep had been a punch to the head that left me bloodied.

I was there because I needed to be there. I was there because I had put it off; I had always stated I didn't have the money or time; it was indulgent and foolish. I told a buddy that I was on the edge of collapse, and she offered me a woman's phone number to call. I'd run out of excuses.

I said, "I think I'm going to fall and die." Eleanor peeked over her spectacles, then returned to her page, furiously jotting notes. She had a dark, semi-parted 70s-style flicky fringe, brown feline eyes, and a powerful nose. She must have been in her early forties. She resembled a young Lauren Hutton. I saw that her arms were muscular, tanned, and graceful. I assumed she thought I was a foolish crybaby. A big fat loser. An overprivileged girl squandering all of her hard-earned money so she could brag about herself for an hour every week. She undoubtedly spotted women like me coming from a mile away.

'I can't open or close any windows in my flat; I have to ask someone else to do it,' I said, clipped and quiet to hold back tears that felt like they were pressing up against the back wall of my eyeballs like water against a flood barrier. 'Sometimes I can't enter a room if a window is open because I'm afraid of falling out. When a train arrives at a tube station from the tunnel, I must stand with my back against the wall. I imagine myself falling in front of it and dying. I can see it happening every time I blink. Then I'll spend the entire night replaying it in my thoughts, unable to sleep.

'Right,' she responded with an Australian accent. 'How long have you felt this way?'

'It's been pretty awful in the last six months,' I explained. But it's been on and off for the better part of a decade. When I'm anxious, I drink excessively. Similarly, there is a fixation with death. Fixation on the flavor of the month is on the decline.

I walked her through the highlights of my recurring emotional turmoil. I discussed my weight, which had been as fluctuating as cloud formations, and how I could look at every photo of myself taken since 2009 and tell her exactly how much I weighed in each one. I told her about my obsession with alcohol that hadn't waned since I was a teenager, my unquenchable thirst when most people my age now knew when to stop, how I'd always been known for knocking it back at record speed, the vast black holes in my memory from these nights over the years, my increasing shame and distress over these lost hours, and that unrecognizable madwoman running around town who I was supposed to be responsible for, but who I had no recollection of being or

I told her about my unwillingness to commit to a relationship, my preoccupation with male attention, and my fear of becoming too close to someone. How painful it had been to watch all of my friends, one by one, ease into long-term relationships as if they were lowering themselves into a cool swimming pool on a hot day. How every partner I'd had had wondered why I couldn't do the same, and how I'd always suspected that I was romantically wired incorrectly.

We discussed how I had spread myself like the final spoonful of Marmite across the breadth of as many lives as possible. I informed her that I donated practically all of my energy to others even though no one had asked for it. I expressed how I thought this gave me power over what others thought of me, but it only made me feel more like a fraud. I told her that I fantasized about what people said about me behind my back, and that I would probably consent to practically any insult thrown at me. I told her about the extremes I had gone to get approval: spending all of my money on rounds of drinks for people I'd never met and not being able to pay my rent the next week; starting Saturday nights at four p.m. and ending them at four a.m. to attend six separate birthday parties of people I hardly knew. This made me feel exhausted, heavy, spineless, and self-loathing. The tragic irony was that I had the best people around me, but I felt unable to tell them anything. How deeply ingrained my fear of dependency was. That I could cry in the bed of a stranger I met in New York but couldn't seek my best friends for assistance.

'But none of this is having a discernible impact on my life,' I stated. 'I feel silly for coming here because things could be a lot worse. I have fantastic friends and a wonderful family. My job is progressing great. No one would notice anything wrong with me from the outside. I simply feel terrible all the time.

'If you feel bad all the time,' she remarked, 'it's having a huge impact on your life.'

'I suppose.'

'You feel like you're about to fall because you're broken into a hundred different floating bits,' she explained. 'You are all over the place. You have no rooting. You do not know how to be with oneself. The back wall of my eyes eventually gave way, and tears streamed from the deepest abyss in the pit of my stomach.

"I feel like nothing is holding me together any longer," I told her, my breathlessness punctuating my phrase like hiccups, the torrent of tears on my cheeks as hot and free-flowing as blood.

'Of course you do,' she replied with new warmth. 'You have no feeling of self.'

So that is why I was there. The realization hit me. I believed I was afraid of falling, but in reality I didn't know who I was. And the things I tried to fill that empty space no longer worked; they only made me feel more disconnected from myself. This overpowering fear had been in the mail for a while, and it had finally arrived, fluttered through the postal box, and dropped on my feet. This diagnosis astonished me since I had assumed my sense of self was rock strong. I am Generation Sense of Self, and this is what we do. We've been filling out 'About Me' sections since 2006. I thought I was the most sensitive selfie taker I knew.

'You'll never know what I truly think of you,' she murmured as I was about to leave, letting me know she'd already noticed how I worked. 'You might be able to tell by my demeanor if I like you, but you'll never know exactly how I feel about you on a personal level. You must let rid of that concept if we are to make any progress.

I experienced an uncomfortable paranoia at first, followed by an almost immediate sense of complete relief. She was instructing me to quit telling bad jokes. She was ordering me to stop apologizing for going through her Kleenex supply on the table next to me. She was telling me that this was a room where I didn't have to labor over every word, gesture, and anecdote in the hopes that she'd appreciate it. This lady, with no sense of self, self-regard, or self-esteem - a shapeshifting, people-pleasing presence; a twisted knot of anxiety - was being allowed to simply be. She was telling me that I was safe to let go in this room right behind Oxford Circus, with the white carpet and burgundy sofa.

I left her office and walked five and a half kilometers home. I felt simultaneously liberated by the relief of having finally finding my way to that chamber and oppressed by the weight of what lay ahead. I assured myself that everything could be resolved in three months.

'She thinks I have no sense of self,' I informed India as she prepared our meal that evening.

'That's rubbish,' she said indignantly. 'You have a more powerful feeling of self than anyone I know.'

'Yeah, but not the sense of self,' I replied. 'Not, for example, how I plan to vote in the EU referendum or how I prefer to serve potatoes. She is referring to the fact that instead of being entire, I divide myself into several parts to provide other individuals. I'm so restless and unsettled. I don't know how to function without all of the things I rely on for support.

'I had no idea you felt this way.'

I told her, 'I feel like I'm falling apart.

'I don't want you to feel unhappy,' India said, holding me barefoot in our kitchen while the spaghetti simmered on the stove, gently boiling. I don't want you to do this if it will make you sad.

The next Friday, I informed Eleanor that India had told me she did not want me to go through this process because she was concerned it would make me sad. I informed her that I was only partially agreeing.

'OK, well, news flash,' she said in her reassuringly straightforward, sarcastic tone, which I would learn to like as the year progressed. 'You are already sad. You are very fucking sad.'

'I know,' I said, grabbing for the Kleenex again. Sorry for using all of these. I guess you go through a lot in your area of business. She told me that was exactly what they were there for.

And so the process started. Every week, I walked in and we conducted detective work on myself to figure out how I got to be the person I am today after 27 years. We conducted a forensic investigation into my past, sometimes discussing something that happened the night before and sometimes something that happened at school in a PE class twenty years ago. Therapy is a huge archaeological dig into your psyche until you find anything. It's a personal weekly edition of Time Team, a collaboration between specialist and presenter - the therapist, Mick

Aston, and the patient, Tony Robinson.

We discussed and talked until she proposed a cause-and-effect hypothesis that suited; then, most importantly, we figured out how to change it. She would sometimes assign me tasks: things to try, things to work on, questions to answer, ideas to chew over, and conversations I needed to have. For two months, I cried every Friday afternoon. Every Friday night, I slept ten hours.

The main fallacy of therapy is that it's all about blaming others; but, as the weeks progressed, I discovered the reverse to be true. I heard about some people's therapists who played a defensive, deluded mother figure in their patients' lives, always reminding them that it was not their fault, but the fault of the lover, boss, or best friend. Eleanor rarely allowed me shift responsibility to someone else and always encouraged me to evaluate what I had done to get myself into a poor situation, which is why I hated our sessions. 'Unless someone dies,' she informed me one Friday, 'if something awful happens in a relationship, you have a role in it.'

A few months later, Eleanor and I finally laughed together for the first time. I came in a shambles after a difficult work week. I was short on money and self-esteem, worried about paying rent, and concerned that my job was going nowhere. My paranoia was out of control; I assumed that everyone I'd ever worked for thought I was incompetent, untalented, and useless. I didn't leave my flat for three days. I detailed to her a vivid nightmare in which a boardroom full of people I didn't know discussed how bad and inadequate I was as a writer. She gazed at me as I spoke, then contorted her face in amazement.

'I mean,' she exclaimed, raising her brow, 'I think it's absurd that you believe that.' I noticed that as she got harder, she became more generally, brashly Australian. I looked up from my tissue; not the reaction I had hoped for.

'Whole boardrooms of people you've never met?' she asked, shaking her head in surprise. 'That is incredibly narcissistic.'

'Well,' I replied, trying to snort with laughter. 'Yeah. When you put it that way. It's ridiculous.'

'Nobody is talking about you.'

'Yeah,' I murmured, patting my tears with the tissue, suddenly feeling like a character from a Woody Allen film. 'You're correct.'

'Seriously!' she exclaimed, still stunned, pulling her fringe away from her high cheeks. 'You're not very intriguing, Dolly.'

In my third month, I had my first tear-free session. The box of Kleenex remained untouched. A therapeutic milestone.

While my closest friends were supportive of the process, it quickly became clear that self-examination made me dull to certain people. I began to drink less and less, constantly doubting if I was doing it for fun or to distract myself from a problem. I attempted to quit people-pleasing, knowing that giving up so much of my time and energy was chipping away at the gap that I didn't want to develop into a quarry. I was more honest; I informed people when I was upset, insulted, or angry, and I cherished the peace of mind that came with integrity, even if it meant having an uncomfortable conversation. As I became more self-aware, I unavoidably made fun of myself for the pleasure of others significantly less.

I felt like I was expanding week after week; I could feel my insides photosynthesizing with each day I practiced new routines. I acquired an indoor plant obsession—a verdant pitiful delusion. I researched what I should put in every spot of light and shadow, and I filled my apartment with green; pothos plants slid down bookshelves, a Boston fern stood on top of my fridge, and a Swiss cheese plant fanned against my brilliant, white bedroom wall. I hung a flawless philodendron over my bed, and at night, the odd icy droplet of water dripped from the heart-shaped apex of its leaves and onto my head. India and Belle questioned how beneficial this was for me, likening it to Chinese water torture. But I'd heard that it was guttation, a process in which a plant drains excess water at night, placing pressure on its roots. I told them it meant something to me. Me and the philodendron were doing something together.

'Any more plants in here?' Farly commented one day, glancing around my bedroom, 'And it's going to turn into Little Shop of Horrors.'

When I didn't drink as much, I had the novel sensation of waking up with a linear memory of the night. People's words, the way they looked, and the discreet messages they exchanged. I realized that everytime I showed up at a social gathering, folks wanted the nasty stuff. If they were at the pub table, they wanted another bottle of wine, to phone a drug dealer, to sit outside and chain smoke, or to drunkenly swap ugly gossip about someone we knew. On a night out, I unknowingly transformed into a black-market trader. I was everyone's green light for terrible behavior, and I had no idea until I stopped.

Eleanor delivered her most ruthless and clever takedown as we were discussing this on Friday afternoon.

'People want me to gossip, I've noticed,' I informed her. 'It's what they expect from me when I get somewhere, especially if they're in disarray.'

And did you gossip?

'A little, yes,' I responded. "I hadn't realized how much I used to do it."

'Why did you do that?'

I don't know. To feel close to others. To have a conversation? Maybe to feel powerful,' I explained. 'That is the sole reason people gossip. I clearly did it to feel powerful.

'Yes, you did,' she responded, smiling slightly, as if happy that I had arrived before her. 'It's pushing them down so you can feel powerful.'

'Yes, I suppose so.'

Do you know anyone else does that? There was a pause. 'Donald Trump.' I burst into laughter.

'Eleanor. I have grown to enjoy your brand of rough love,' I informed her. "But even for you, that is a bit of a stretch."

'Fine, a Nigel Farage then,' she remarked, shrugging slightly, as if I was being picky.

I texted Farly, "My therapist compared me to Donald Trump today," as I went out into Regent Street. 'I believe I am making significant progress.'

Then, about five months into therapy, I felt like we had struck a brick wall. My progress stalled. I found myself getting protective towards her. She told me that I was becoming defensive with her. In one session, I offered that there might not be an answer in dissecting my life's events and decisions; in going over and over what happened with that lover once or what my parents did or did not say when I was growing up. That perhaps it was a pointless exercise; that perhaps I was simply born this way. Did she believe there was a chance I was born this way? She looked at me blankly.

She said, "No, I don't."

'Well, obviously you don't,' I answered in a sour tone. 'Because otherwise, your job would be completely unnecessary.'

If I messed up that week, I would occasionally plan out a tale to tell her so she wouldn't be too harsh on me. Then I realized how much I was spending to see her, all the additional work I'd had to do to afford it, and how fortunate I was to be able to afford it at all. And what a waste of money if I hadn't told her the truth. I chatted with some acquaintances in analysis who stated they were apprehensive before their sessions because they were trying to think of something tasty to tell the therapist. I felt the complete opposite. I was always thinking about what I could hide from her or how I might put a positive spin on a story to make it appear less horrible than it was.

But she always saw straight through it. Because I'd told her how I worked. I always despised how well she knew me, and when she challenged me, I would fall into tears. I didn't dislike her for questioning what I'd done; I disliked myself for doing it in the first place.

At six months, I almost said, "What makes YOU so fucking wise about all this stuff?" Come on. Tell me how perfect you are during a session. I realized I needed to take a vacation from it, but I didn't tell her. She said she'sensed some wrath', but I told her I was alright. I began cancelling sessions. I missed a month and a half.

When I returned to her, I discovered she was lot more understanding than I remembered, and I wondered if I had imagined her tenacious and unforgiving line of inquiry. Perhaps she had become a blank canvas on which I could project all of my rage and self-judgment. In the middle of our hour together, she asked me why I had stopped visiting on a regular basis without first discussing it with her. I considered fabricating an excuse, thinking about the money and time I was investing in this, and how it was too late to back out now.

'I don't know,' I replied.

'Is it because it's becoming too intimate?' she inquired. 'Is this a dependency issue? "You don't want to depend on this?"

'Yeah,' I replied, sighing. 'I think that's it; I believe I wanted to control it.'

'Yeah, I guess that could be it,' she answered, thinking aloud. 'What's happening in your outer life is reflected in here.'

'It makes sense.

What are you trying to control?

'Everything,' I realized as I stated it aloud. I'm attempting to influence everyone's view of me. How everyone acts towards me. I'm attempting to prevent negative things from happening. Death, calamity, and disappointment. I'm trying to keep everything under control.

Her epiphany was my epiphany, and I chose to give in to the process. I passed myself up to Eleanor with trust, and we began a new cycle of time together.

She told me, 'You need to keep coming here, and we need to keep talking. "We need to talk and talk and talk until we get everything together."

I believe part of the difficulty was that I couldn't face Eleanor learning so much about me - the darkest caverns of who I am, my most sacred, embarrassing, humiliating, horrific, and beautiful events. And I received nothing about her in return. Sometimes I envisioned Eleanor at home, wondering what her life would be like if she wasn't a therapist. I wondered what she said about me to her friends, whether she ever read my articles, checked my social media feeds, or googled me, like I did the first time I received an invoice with her complete name on it.

A few weeks later, she inquired how I was doing with treatment, and I admitted that I despised not knowing anything about her. I informed her that while I understood that this was the proper exchange, I sometimes thought that it was unjust. Why did I have to be naked every week while she always got to be fully clothed?

'What do you mean, you don't know anything about me?' she inquired, clearly perplexed.

'I know nothing about you personally.'

'Yes, you do,' she replied.

'No, I can't tell my friends anything about you.'

'You come in here every week, and we speak about love, sex, family, friendship, happiness, and sadness. You know exactly what I believe about all of these issues.

But I'm not sure if you're married, if you have children, or where you reside. I'm not sure where you go out. I'm not sure if you go to the gym,' I added, thinking primarily of her toned arms, which I usually found myself admiring in particularly difficult periods and wondering what weights she used.

'Do you think understanding any of that will help you grasp who I am?' she inquired. 'You know so much about me.'

Over time, I learned Eleanor's language. After a particularly tearful session, she always emphasized, 'Take good care' - emphasis on the 'good'. That indicated, 'Don't get too leathered this weekend. It was also unfortunate that she said 'Oh boy' when I told her something. The worst, by far, was 'I've been worrying about you this week.' Eleanor mentioned she was worried about me that week, which meant I had put on a real shit show the previous Friday.

I never stopped dreading Fridays, although I did so less and less. Eleanor and I laughed more together. I told her that occasionally after our sessions, I went directly to Pret and ate a brownie in about five seconds flat, or I walked into a shop and bought something for ten quid that I didn't need. She explained that it was because I was concerned about what she thought of me, and I agreed. It's not natural to sit in a small room with someone who isn't a part of your life and give them all of your raw, unedited stories - the ones you've never told anyone, including yourself. But as I got healthy, I felt less judgment towards her. Her full form began to emerge in front of me: a woman who was on my side.

I realized when a friend informed me that healing is brought about by the relationship between the patient and the therapist, not by the talking. My gradual sensation of quiet and contentment felt like something we were creating together, like a physio who developed a muscle. I kept a small piece of her with me, and I'm sure I always will. The work helped me gain a new awareness of myself, which I will never be able to deny or bury. She termed it 'the work'. And that's how it always felt. My time with Eleanor was challenging, confronting, and difficult. She did not allow me to get away with anything. She made me reflect on the role I played in everything. I sometimes tried to recall a time when my actions had no ramifications; after particularly painful Friday afternoons, I wondered what life would be like if I hadn't opted to embark on this journey into myself. Would it have been easier to just continue being a drunk jackass in a taxi driving down the M1 at four a.m.? A person whose behavior was ignored and then repeated the following weekend?

Eleanor used to tell me that life is awful. She informed me every week. She said it would disappoint me. She reminded me that there was nothing I could do to prevent it. I accepted the inevitable.

As we approached our one-year anniversary, our chats became more familiar and comfortable; she selected literature she believed I would find useful. She generally said 'Goodbye' rather than 'Take good care'. She stopped responding 'Oh no' in a concerned tone when I told her a story, and I began hearing a truly joyful 'Well, this all sounds GREAT!' on a regular basis. One Friday, I truly ran out of things to tell her.

I wasn't sure how long I wanted to spend there or how free I wanted to feel. But I knew that the more I stayed there, the more things came together. I persuaded myself into harmony, exactly as she prophesied.

I linked the dots and found the patterns. The discourse began to connect with the action. The difference between how I felt inside and how I behaved narrowed. When things went wrong, I learned to dwell with them, to go profoundly, uncomfortably inward, rather than to the Outer Hebrides of Experience. The drinking became less often, and when it did, it was done for celebration rather than escape, so the effect was never devastating.

I felt steadier and stronger. I unlocked the doors inside me one by one, emptied the rooms of all my stuff, and talked her through every piece of old toot I found in there before throwing it all out. Each room I opened brought me closer. A sense of self, a sense of tranquility. There is also a sense of home.

HEARTBREAK HOTEL

I awoke to three missed calls from Farly before 7 a.m., as well as a message urging me to call her. Before I could dial her number, she called again. I knew it was not good. I reflected on the last eighteen months since Florence's death, and how Farly had isolated herself from all of her closest friends, burying her sadness in the distance. How I had attempted to entice her back to me, to know what to say to comfort her. When we'd laugh about something and I'd catch a glimpse of her former personality, the laughter would change to deep tears, and she'd apologize for not understanding how her complete mind or body was functioning any longer. Selfishly, I had only one thought: I'm not sure how I'll get her through this again. I took a deep breath before picking up the phone.

'Dolly?'

'What has happened?'

'No one has died,' she answered, noticing the panic in my voice.

'OK.'

'This is Scott. I believe we're breaking up.

It was eight weeks until their wedding.

When I arrived an hour later, Farly was alone in their flat; Scott had left for work, and her manager had granted her a few days of compassionate leave. She walked me through their chat from the night before, minute by moment. She informed me that she had not expected this, that the wedding was the least of her concerns right now, and that she would go to any length to maintain her love. Her father and stepmother were spending the weekend in Cornwall, so we drove down there so she and Scott could have some alone time to contemplate.

We planned out what she wanted to say to him over the phone. When he called, she requested if I could sit in the same room with her since she was nervous and needed someone in her eyeline to keep her calm. I sat on their sofa as she moved around their flat on the phone, admiring the place they shared and the life they'd created together. There was a snapshot of them in their early and mid-twenties, lovingly holding each other; it was from their last holiday with Florence. The burnt-orange rug I assisted them in selecting; the sofa on which the three of us sipped red wine till dawn while watching election results on television. The Morrissey print we purchased for their engagement is hanging on the wall.

I had an unusual and difficult thinking. For many years, this was all I wanted. I used to hope that one of them would eventually separate from the other, that we'd always talk warmly of Scott the First Love, and that I'd reclaim my best buddy. But now that moment had arrived, and all I could feel was wrenching pain and love for her. They'd been through so much together, and I desperately wanted them to sort things out.

We had all imagined Farly and Scott's approaching wedding as a type of Polyfilla for the void left in their family. Whenever her family or any of our friends discussed what the day would be like, we all agreed it would be filled with both immense soaring elation and unavoidable pain - but it would undoubtedly mark a new chapter in their life. A beginning rather than a finish.

Following Florence's death, I assumed the role of maid of honor with the gravitas of a knighthood. AJ, Lacey, and I planned a hen do with the same ambition and scale as the Olympic Opening Ceremony. After months of petitioning and negotiating, an East London hotel gave us their top-floor event space overlooking the city at a much reduced rate to throw a large dinner. I arranged for the London Gay Men's Chorus to perform a surprise set of wedding-related songs for Farly while wearing T-shirts with her face printed. I collaborated with a mixologist to create The Farly cocktail. I ordered a life-size cardboard cut-out man from eBay and attached a photo of Scott's face so that others could take photos with him. I taped dozens of video messages from individuals wishing her well in her marriage to show on the night, similar to a This Is Your Life VT. These included Dean Gaffney, a 1990s EastEnders actor, two Made in Chelsea cast members, the boy she lost her virginity to, and the boss of her local dry cleaners.

I went back to the conversation she was having with Scott.

'Perhaps the wedding was too huge,' she replied. 'Do you know? Maybe we let the wedding spiral out of control. Maybe we should just forget about everything and focus on ourselves.

At that very time, I received an email from Farly's local MP's office.

Dear Dolly,

Thank you for your email. Andy would be delighted to help – it sounds like you are going above and beyond to make sure your friend has a very special hen do! Would you be able to pop by Andy's constituency office next Monday at 11.30 a.m. to film?

If that isn't convenient, I will have a look in his diary to find another day.

Best wishes,

Kristin

I removed it silently.

We drove up to my flat, where I threw a few things in a suitcase and texted India and Belle to let them know Farly had tonsillitis and Scott was away for work, so I'd be staying with her for a few days. I felt awful about lying, but because everything was still up in the air and no final decision had been made, it was best to keep things ambiguous so she wouldn't ask any questions. I set up an out-of-office message, and we drove to Cornwall.

We'd taken the M25, M4, and M5 several times before. For holidays at the house in Cornwall, summer road trips when we were sixteen and seventeen, and trips back and forth from London to Exeter when we were at university. Farly had a strict rating system for all motorway service stations based on their snack options, and she enjoyed testing me on her preferred order (Chieveley, Heston, Leigh Delamere).

Strangely, a long vehicle drive felt like just what we needed at the time. Her automobile was the foundation of our adolescent romance. Farly's driver's license was our ticket to freedom during the years when I desperately wanted to be an adult. It was our first shared flat; it was our refuge from the outside world. There was a vista on a hill in Stanmore that looked out over the glittering metropolis like it was Oz. We'd travel there after school, share a package of Silk Cut and a tub of Ben & Jerry's, and listen to Magic FM.

'What do you see when you look at that?' she asked me a few weeks before we finished school.

'I see all the boys I'll fall in love with, the novels I'll write, the flats I'll live in, and the days and nights that await me. What do you see?

'Something absolutely terrifying,' she responded.

The five-hour drive felt longer than usual. Perhaps because it wasn't accompanied by chit-chat, radio, or scratched Joni Mitchell CDs, but rather a silence that wasn't a silence; I could hear the noise in Farly's thoughts. We rested her phone on the dashboard and waited for Scott to call and admit he had made a terrible mistake. Every time her phone turned on, her gaze shifted from the road to the screen.

'Check it for me,' she would ask hurriedly. It was always another message from one of our friends, wishing her and her tonsillitis well and asking if they might come over with soup and magazines.

'For fuck's sake,' she exclaimed, managing a faint laugh. 'Me and him have spent the last six years texting continuously about the most boring things, and now all I want is to hear from him, but all I get is a slew of texts of support about a fabricated sickness.'

'At least you know you are loved,' I said. There was more uneasy quiet.

'What am I going to tell everyone?" she inquired. 'All the wedding guests.'

'You don't need to think about it yet,' I added. 'And if that case arises, you will not have to tell anyone anything. We can do it all for you.

'I don't know how I would live this without you,' she replied. 'As long as I have you, everything will be fine.'

'I am right here,' I told her. 'I am not going anywhere. I'll be here for you forever, mate. And we'll make it to the other side together, no matter what that location looks like.

Tears streamed down her cheeks as she gazed directly ahead into the darkness of the M5.

'I apologize if I ever made you feel like you were second best, Dolly.'

When we arrived shortly after midnight, Richard and Annie were waiting for us. I made tea - in the week after Floss died, I memorized how everyone drank theirs; it was the only useful thing I could do - and we sat on the sofa, going over everything that had been said and the probable possibilities.

Farly and I lay in the same bed with the lights turned off.

"Do you know what the real tragedy in all this is?"

'Go ahead,' she said.

'Me and Lauren have finally mastered all of the chords and harmonies of "One Day Like This" for the ceremony.'

'Oh, I understand; don't. I loved the recording you sent me.'

'And the string quartet has just verified they can do the introduction.'

'I know.'

'It might be a blessing in disguise,' I explained. 'I genuinely believe that song makes everyone think about X Factor montages today.'

'Will you lose money on the hen do?'

'Don't worry about it,' I responded. 'We'll work things out.' There was silence in the darkness while I waited for her next sentence.

'Go ahead,' she said. 'I'm 90% certain it's not occurring now, so you may as well tell me.'

But will it make you sad?

"No, it will cheer me up."

I informed her about the weekend we had planned for her. She grumbled with each ludicrous detail, like a child who had missed out on chocolates. We watched films on my phone of the Great and the Good of Britain's D-List wishing each other well.

'Thank you for planning it,' she replied. It would have been fantastic. I would've liked it.

'We will do it for you all again.'

'I will not marry again.'

'You don't realize that. Even if you don't, I'll simply postpone all of those arrangements until a birthday. I'll do you a fantastic fortieth." I heard her breathing deepen and slow; after years of bed-sharing and fussing about her falling asleep before the end of a movie, I knew she was dozing off. 'Wake me up at night if you need me,' I added.

'Thank you, Dolls. "I wish we could just be in a relationship sometimes," she remarked, sleepily. 'Everything would be easy.'

'Yeah, but you're not my type, Farley.'

She laughed for a few minutes before crying. I rubbed her back without saying anything.

The following several days were spent going for long walks, going over the identical facts of their last conversation over and over again, attempting to figure out where things went wrong. I made tea that Farly didn't drink, Richard prepared meals that she scarcely ate, and we watched TV while she stared into the middle distance. After a few days, I needed to return to London for work. Farly returned to the city a few days later, and she and Scott arranged to meet in their neighborhood park for a walk and to talk about everything.

On the morning of their meeting, I couldn't concentrate on anything and stared at my phone like it was a television, waiting for her message. Finally, three hours later, I decided to phone her. She grabbed up before the first ring was completed.

'It's over,' she announced hastily. Tell everyone that the wedding is off. I will call you later.

The telephone went dead.

I called our close friends one by one and described what had happened; each was as astonished as the last. I carefully drafted a message stating that the wedding was cancelled and sent it to Farly's half of the guest list. And suddenly it was finished. Extinguished by copying and pasting a message into an email and making a few phone calls. Their story ended on that day in the future. I removed every complex component of her hen do, which was scheduled to take place in less than a month, and cancelled it all. Everyone I called, who knew the wedding had been postponed a year due to a family tragedy, said nothing but their condolences.

Farly left the flat the day of their chat to stay with Annie and Richard at their family home a few miles away. I arrived at home with my positive bank account completely depleted and my overdraft of cheering platitudes running deep.

She told me, "I feel like I'm in jail for something I didn't do." 'I feel like my life is someplace over there, and I'm trapped in here, told I can't get there. "I want my old life back."

'You will get there. I promise that it will not be like this forever.

'I am cursed.'

'No,' I replied. 'You are not cursed. You've had a horrific, excruciating run of bad luck. You've experienced more darkness in eighteen months than most people do in a lifetime. But you've got so much light ahead of you; you've got to hold on to it.

That was what everyone said after Florence died. I do not think I can take much more.

With everyone's encouragement, Farly returned to work right away, and our pals launched a military effort to keep her distracted into activity. Even though it was the most time we'd spent together since we were teenagers, I also wrote her postcards every other day to ensure she always had something beautiful to come home to after work. The bridesmaids took her out for a weekend of wine and cooking in the countryside for her hen party. I planned us a trip to Sardinia for the week of her wedding. We all took turns spending the evenings with her after work in the month following their breakup; there wasn't a night that went by without at least one of us present. Sometimes we talked about what was going on, and sometimes we just sat there eating Lebanese takeout and watching trashy TV. On the way home, whoever visited would send a message to the rest of us to let us know how she was doing and who was going to see her next. We were a circle of keepers, nurses on shift. Our first-aid kit contained Maltesers and episodes of Gogglebox.

It was at this point that I was reminded of the chain of support that keeps a sufferer afloat: the person in the center of a crisis requires the support of their family and best friends, who in turn require support from their friends, partners, and family. Then even those folks twice removed may need to speak with someone about it. It takes a village to heal a broken heart.

I drove back to the flat with Farly and waited in the car while she collected more of her items and had one last conversation with Scott. Their apartment went on the market. Farly unpacked her belongings into her childhood bedroom, which was now more than temporary but less than permanent.

The first time any of us saw an ember of Farly's old personality was on a completely catastrophic Sunday when I roped my friends into organizing a picture shoot for a faux dinner party. It was to complement an article I wrote for a broadsheet culture section about the demise of the traditional dinner party, and the editor requested a photograph of me 'entertaining guests' at my flat. I'd informed him that I didn't have any male friends available that day, and he reluctantly agreed that an all-female gathering would suffice. However, when the photographer arrived, it appeared that he had received new instructions to ensure that there were guys in the photo.

Farly, who had been drinking white wine since lunchtime, went door-to-door along my street, hoping to find a receptive male neighbour, but was unsuccessful. Meanwhile, Belle and AJ drove to our neighborhood bar, went inside, tapped a glass to get everyone's attention, and made a pretty lame statement that they were searching for a few men to be photographed in exchange for some slow-roast lamb and a picture in the paper.

'If this sounds interesting to you,' Belle said, 'then we'll be waiting outside in the red Seat Ibiza.'

Five minutes later, a group of sweaty and drunken guys in their thirties and forties emerged from the tavern and entered the car.

When we were all crammed around the table, clinking glasses and pretending to be old friends, it became evident that one of the gentlemen was far more inebriated than the rest, eating the roast lamb with his hands like a Roman emperor. The photographer was standing on a chair to get all of us in the image in my pretty tiny living room when a light broke and one of the men began yelling for more wine. It was a slapstick caper in which people ran around and objects broke with low-level frenzied energy.

'This is a disaster,' I whispered quietly to the females.

'Oh, I don't believe it's a disaster AT ALL,' Farly exclaimed drunkenly. "I got jilted by my boyfriend of seven years a month ago, so this is a walk in the park!" The photographer looked at me for reassurance, and the drunken emperor stopped masticating. 'Cheers,' she exclaimed cheerfully, raising her glass to each of us.

We rapidly learned how to deal with this type of suicide bomb of a joke, which became a common and well-worn piece of furniture in our interactions with Farly. You couldn't participate in the discussion because you didn't know where the black comedy ended and tipped over into cruelty; but, you couldn't ignore it. You just had to chuckle aloud.

We left for Sardinia a few days before Farly's wedding date. We arrived late and drove up to the north-west of the island in our uninsured rental car, carefully winding up coastal roads with the same Joni Mitchell song in the stereo that we'd played on our first road trip almost ten years before. A time when a relationship seemed ridiculously out of reach, let alone a canceled wedding.

We slept at a really simple hotel with a pool, a bar, and a room with a view of the sea; that was all we required. Farly, the girl who loved school and went on to become a teacher, is and has always been a creature who follows a schedule, so we immediately formed our own. Every morning, we awoke early and went straight to the beach to workout in the dazzling, white light of the early sun, followed by a dip in the water before breakfast. Well, I would swim. Farly would sit in the sand and watch. Farly and I disagree the most on the matter of outdoor swimming; I strip off at the sight of almost any body of open water for a dip, whereas Farly only swims in chlorinated pools.

'Come on!' I yelled at the shore one morning, when the sea was calm and pleasant as bathwater. 'You need to come in! It's really wonderful.

'But what if there are fish?' she yelled at me grimly.

'There are no fish!' I raised my voice. 'All okay, there could be some fish.'

'You know I'm afraid of fish,' she shouted back.

'How can you be terrified of them? You eat them.'

'I don't like the idea of them swimming underneath me.'

'You sound so damned suburban, Farly,' I exclaimed at her. "You don't want to miss out on life because you only shop in malls because you're afraid of rain ruining your blow-dry, and you only swim in pools because you're afraid of fish."

'We're suburban, Dolly. That's literally who we are.

'Come on!' It is natural! It's God's swimming pool! It is healing! God is in the ocean!

'If there's one thing I know for certain,' she rose up and wiped the sand from her legs, 'it's that there is no God, Doll! She yelled it joyously as she paddled into the sea.

We'd spend the morning reading books and listening to music, then have our first drink of the day about midday. We dozed all afternoon in the sun before showering and going out to supper in town. We'd return to the hotel, sip Amaretto Sours on the patio under the thick blanket of nighttime heat, play cards, and send tipsy postcards to our friends.

Farly woke up before I did on the wedding day. She stared at the ceiling.

'Are you okay?' I asked the moment my eyes opened.

'Yeah,' she replied, turning aside and lifting the cover. "I just want today to be over."

'Today will be one of the most difficult days,' I added. 'And then it will be completed. It ends at midnight. And you won't have to go through that again.

'Yeah,' she replied gently. I sat at the end of her bed.

'What would you like to do today?' I inquired. 'I've reserved a restaurant for tonight that has fantastic five-star Trip Advisor reviews with awful close-up images of the food like it's a crime scene.'

'That sounds fine,' she murmured with a sigh. 'I suppose I just want to lay on a beach lounger like a simple bitch.'

We spent the majority of the day in silence, reading books and listening to podcasts together through earplugs. She would occasionally look around and remark things like, 'I'd be having breakfast with my bridesmaids now,' or 'I'd probably be putting on my wedding dress.' She took up her phone about mid-afternoon and checked the time.

It's ten to four in England. I would have been married in exactly ten minutes.

'Yeah, but at least you're here sunning in lovely Italy, not floating down a lake with your dad in wet Oxfordshire.

'I was never going to arrive by gondola,' she remarked exasperatedly. 'I only mentioned it as an option because the venue stated that's what some of the other brides had done.

'You did consider it, however.'

No, I didn't.

'Yes, because when you told me about it, I could tell you were waiting for me to say if I thought it was a good idea.'

No, I wasn't!

'It would have been so embarrassing, everyone watching at you as you floated down a lake in a gigantic dress, then someone yanking you out of it, the sailor clattering around with the oars.

'It did not have a sailor,' she complained. 'And it did not have oars.'

I went into the bar and ordered a bottle of Prosecco.

'Right,' I replied, pouring the ice-cold fizz into poolside plastic flutes.

'You would have made vows by now. I believe we should make vows.

'To whom?'

'To ourselves,' I explained. And to each other.

'OK,' she replied, placing her sunglasses on top of her head. 'You go first.'

'I swear not to judge how you handle this when we go home,' I added. 'If you want to have a very heavy amphetamine and casual sex phase, that's OK. If you lock yourself in your house for a year, that's alright. You have my full support in anything you do, since I cannot understand what it must be like to lose the people you have.

'Thank you,' she replied, sipping her Prosecco and pausing to consider.

I promise to always let you grow. I will never tell you that I know who you truly are simply because we have known one other since we were children. I realize you're going through a tremendous shift, and I'll always encourage you.

'That's a good one,' I replied, clinking her glass. 'Okay, I will always notify you when you have something in your teeth.'

'Oh, always.'

Especially as we get older and our gums begin to recede. That's when the leafy greens can truly become lodged.

'Don't make me more depressed than I already am,' she pleaded.

Make a pledge to yourself.

"I vow to never lose sight of my friends if I fall in love again," she remarked. "I'll never forget how important you are and how much we need each other."

On the night of Farly's wedding reception for over 200 people, we took a taxi to a hilltop restaurant with a view of the sea.

'You would have been giving your speech now,' she replied. 'Have you ever written it?'

'No,' I replied. Whenever I've felt angry or emotional, I've jotted down some ideas in my iPhone notes. But I hadn't written it up yet.

'I wonder if I would have been joyful all day or if I would have found anything stressful.'

I remembered reading an article on premature death after Florence died, in which an agony aunt encouraged a mourning father not to consider the life his teenage son would have led if he hadn't been killed in a vehicle accident. This fantasy, she claimed, was a form of agony rather than consolation.

'You know, life isn't occurring elsewhere,' I explained. 'It does not exist in another realm. Your relationship with that man lasted seven years. That was all it was.'

'I understand.'

'Your life is right now. You're not going to live in a tracing-paper version of it.

"Yeah, I suppose it's best not to dwell on what could have been."

Don't think of it as sliding doors.

'I adore that flick.'

"And thank God it's not because no one could ever pull off Gwyneth Paltrow's blonde haircut."

'I'd look like Myra Hindley,' Farly stated bluntly, motioning for another carafe of wine. "Did you have doubts about me and him?"

"Do you want to know honestly?"

'Yes, I truly do,' she replied. 'It doesn't matter now, but I'd like to know.

'Yes,' I replied. 'I began to actually love him, and at the end, I believed there was a future in which you might be extremely happy. But, yeah, I have always had reservations.

She stared out at the sinking sun, which sat on the horizon of the deep-blue Mediterranean like a perfectly balanced peach on a ledge.

'Thank you for not telling me.'

The sea swallowed the sun, and the sky gradually faded to dusky blue, then night, as if controlled by a dimmer. There was never another day as horrible as that one.

After a week together, we drove to another coastal town, where Sabrina and Belle greeted us. The vacation continued in the same vein: we drank Aperol, played cards, and relaxed on the beach. Belle and I left the apartment at six a.m. one morning, stripped on the beach, and swam naked in the light of dawn. Farly had both good and bad days during our final week, which was understandable. We all talked a lot about what happened, which was the underlying reason for the holiday. But she also began talking about the future rather than the past; where she was going to live, and what her new routine would be like. Over the course of the fortnight, it felt as if she shed one of her sad layers. One night, she became so inebriated - more so than we'd been since we were teenagers - that she began hitting on the manager of a local restaurant who resembled a sixty-something Italian John Candy; undoubtedly the most recognizable rite of passage and one that indicates you're entering a new phase of getting over a breakup.

When we returned to London, things felt drastically different. Her twenty-ninth birthday came three months after I awoke that morning to three missed calls. It seemed like a milestone, so we celebrated properly: we went to one of our favorite pubs for supper, then went dancing. She donned the dress I had bought for her hen do, which never happened. It was black and cut low on either side, revealing a tattoo she received when she was nineteen, a catastrophic, rash decision in a Watford parlor. Two little stars, one pink and one an unplanned yellow ('A Jew with a yellow star tattooed on her! I beg you!' her mother lamented).

On the afternoon of her birthday, she went to another tattoo shop to correct her mistake from a decade ago. She filled in the stars with dark ink and painted them black. She wrote a 'F' next to one of them for Florence and a 'D' for me. A reminder that no matter what we lose, no matter how uncertain and unpredictable life becomes, certain people truly walk alongside us forever.

I GOT GURUED

Early in the summer of Farly's sadness, I was requested to write a first article for a magazine about the perils of pleasing others. The editor I was working for recommended that I speak with a man who had authored a new book about the subject. His name was David, and he was over fifty. He was an actor turned writer. Before we chatted on the phone, I looked him up on Google and realized he was really attractive: olive skin, salt-and-pepper hair, kind brown eyes. His publisher emailed me a PDF of the book, which was a painfully excellent read. His studies focuses on the human need for affirmation and how it limits enjoyment. Reading it seemed as if something - or someone - had gripped my shoulders with strong, trustworthy hands and given me a good, sharp, much-needed shaking.

We exchanged emails for a while before setting up a time to speak. His voice was deep and velvety, far more prominent and theatrical than I had expected. His overall demeanor appeared to be that of an out-and-out hippie, but he spoke like an RSC ensemble member. I asked him about the book and the aspects that had particularly resonated with me, and he reminded me that as children, we are continually instructed to control our behaviour. He noted how being admonished not to be bossy, not to brag, or not to be clever-clogs creates barriers around certain aspects of ourselves that we are afraid to revisit as adults. Instead, we hide aspects of ourselves that are dark, loud, unusual, or twisted for fear of being disliked. He contended that such aspects of ourselves were the most beautiful.

Because the poem was written from a personal perspective, we had to discuss my own experiences. I informed him that I had started seeing a therapist this year.

'The danger of a somebody like you doing therapy is that you appear clever,' he explained. 'You'll quickly grasp the underlying principles. You'll be able to speak academically about oneself in conversation. But all that talking will only get you so far. That change must be felt deeply within you. It can't just be topics you discuss with your therapist. You must feel it in your body -" his voice softened - "in the backs of your knees, in your womb, in your toes, and in your fingers."

'Hmm,' I agreed.

We talked for around 45 minutes, ranging from book passages to years of research and work he had done, as well as my own experiences. He addressed me frankly, with no formality or civility. I felt as if he had gotten straight to my inner equator via phone call.

'Pinch that small cheek of yours,' he said, like if he'd known me forever. 'You don't need others to tell you what to do or who to be. You are now your own mommy. You must listen to what you want.

'Hm,' I managed again.

"And every day for the rest of your life, I want you to take that job seriously."

But what about being appropriate? How does that work when you are always true to yourself?'

'Have you ever fell in love with a man because he is suitable?'

'Well, no.'

'Oooh, Greg,' he said in a passionate tone. 'He turns me on; he is so fucking appropriate.'

'No, no,' I replied, smiling.

'I am not interested in appropriate. Buried wealth can be found in the dark, at the edges, and in corners. 'Fucking appropriate.

I felt like he was flirting with me, but I couldn't tell if he was speaking to me so intimately just to get good quotations for the article. By the end of our meeting, we had devolved into a broad discussion that seemed nothing like an interview. I could see he wanted me to disclose if I was in a relationship, but I kept it vague. He suggested that I have a one-on-one session with him.

'If you feel like you can show everything of yourself to someone without fear of being criticized, your closeness will skyrocket,' he said.

'Yeah, that has always been a significant problem for me,' I admitted. 'Intimacy.'

'I know; I can feel it in you.' There was a brief hush between us. Maybe he was spouting guru nonsense; perhaps what I had always pushed down was much more evident than I realized.

'Hm,' I managed once more.

'I hope you have someone in your life who truly values you, Dolly.'

'I have a therapist,' I responded.

'That's not what I meant,' he replied.

I stepped out of my flat and blinked into the light, like if I had just woken up.

"I just had the most extraordinary conversation," I told India and Belle, who were sunbathing in our garden.

'With whom?' India inquired, taking her earphones out.

"That guy for the article—that guru guy."

'What did he say?'

'I don't know, it was like he was speaking to something inside me that had never been spoken to before; it was as if something was yawning and waking up for the first time.'

'That's what they do, isn't it? They make you believe that's the power they have,' India remarked sombrely, turning to face her front. 'I would never believe somebody who claimed to be a guru.'

'To be fair, he doesn't call himself a guru,' I explained. 'Everybody else does.'

'OK, that's better,' she said.

'It's similar to being a "maven,"' I continued. Or a "mogul". You have to wait for someone else to say it, I believe. You can't say that about yourself." I removed my top and joined them on the towels they'd put on the grass.

'Did you acquire what you needed from him?' Belle inquired.

'Yes,' I replied. 'He was a fantastic interviewee.' I closed my eyes and allowed the bright English sun give me a rare hug. 'Jesus, I will not be able to stop thinking about him.

'In, like, a sexual way?' India inquired.

'No, I do not think so. I want to eat your soul. I just want to know everything about him, and I want to hear everything he says.

'Ask for his number,' she instructed.

I already have his number. I just interviewed him over the phone.

'Oh yes,' she replied. 'Well, just text him.'

'I can't "just text" someone I interviewed for a story.

Why not?' Belle inquired.

'Because that would be inappropriate,' I explained, catching the words in my mouth. 'But who has fallen in love with appropriate?'

I listened to the recording again in bed that night, his words bouncing about in my head like a ping pong ball. The next morning, I wrote the piece, sent it to the editor, and then forgot about him.

A few months later, while I was returning home late after a party, I received a WhatsApp message from David. He informed me he was on vacation in France and had just gone for a long walk under the stars when he suddenly remembered our interview and realized he hadn't seen it anywhere.

'This is definitely my narcissism speaking; when is the piece coming out?'

'Not narcissistic at all,' I responded. 'I'm sorry, it was postponed due to a problem. I'll text you the day it comes out next month. I can send you a copy if you aren't in the nation.

I'll be back by then. How are you?' he asked. 'You appeared on the verge of something the last time we spoke.'

I typed, 'Still on the edge of something. 'I'm still attempting to transition into a different mindset. Easy-peasy. How are you?'

'Same.'

He informed me that he had recently ended a long-term relationship. He stated that it was the correct thing to do: a mutually agreeable split. He informed me that sometimes a breakup can be nothing more than a relief for both sides, like turning off the air conditioner, the low, constant hum of which you had no idea was there until everything went silent.

We texted for hours that night, learning things about each other that we hadn't discovered in our first discussion. We both grew up in North London and attended orthodox boarding schools, so I figured he despised his voice as much as I despised mine. He had four children, two boys and two girls, and he clearly adored all of them. I could detect a dad using his children as a chat-up line from a mile away, but this was not one. He understood every little detail about each child's personality, passions, dreams, and everyday life, and he spoke about them all with true interest and dedication.

We discussed music and song lyrics. I told him that my favorite artist was John Martyn, and that his music was the only love affair I'd ever had with a man that lasted more than a few years. He told me a tale about how he got one of John Martyn's guitars from his ex-wife and told me I could have it if I wanted, knowing how obsessed I was with his music. We chatted about a book we'd both read that had converted me to vegetarianism; we both got outraged about the same statistics and passages. We chatted about how we spent our childhood holidays in France. We spoke about our parents. We spoke about the rain. I told him how much I adored it—more than blue skies and sunshine. I told him how the rain had always cradled and calmed me, how as a child, I would beg my mother if I might sit in the boot of her car parked outside while it rained. I told him that when I read in Rod Stewart's book that he would stand in the middle of the street with his arms outstretched when it rained once a year in Los Angeles because he missed it so much, I knew I could never leave England. We say goodnight at 3 a.m.

The next morning, I awoke feeling like I was recuperating from a vivid dream. But, sure enough, there was a new message from David on my phone, waiting for me beneath my pillow like a beautiful, shining pound coin from the tooth fairy.

'You woke me up at five this morning,' it read.

What do you mean?' I responded. He emailed me a recording of heavy rain falling on his bedroom window, followed by light rain.

Am I the rain?' I inquired, suspending my well-worn pessimism in a manner that would become a feature of our meetings.

'Yes, you are,' he responded. 'I sensed you move closer.'

I had to tell my pals about David since I could never get off the phone with him. We texted each other from the moment we awoke until we went to bed. I set aside roughly five hours of the day to work, eat, and wash, but even then, I was thinking about him. I had lunch with Sabrina, and she said she could tell I was staring at my phone screen the entire time.

'Okay, enough with the phone,' she said.

'I am not on my phone!I replied defensively.

'You're not physically on your phone, but I can tell you're only thinking about conversing with him.'

'No, I am not.'

'You are, it's like I've taken my thirteen-year-old daughter out for lunch and she wants to be back on MSN Messenger, talking to her foreign exchange student lover.

'I apologize,' I said. 'I promise, I'm not thinking about him.' My phone lit up.

'What has he sent there?' Sabrina inquired, looking down at the screen.

I showed her a photograph of an elaborate illustration of a lion.

'He believes my inner energy is a lion.

Sabrina gave me a couple confused glances.

'Yeah, I don't think we'll have much in common, me and your new partner,' she stated bluntly.

No, you will. He's not a solemn, humourless guru; he's quite humorous.

'OK, just slow down the texting,' she added. 'Please. For your sake.

You're going to wreck your relationship before it ever begins. He reminds me of a human Tamagotchi.

'But he's in France for three weeks,' I explained. 'I'm not going to stop speaking to him until he returns and we can meet.'

'Oh my God, I bet he instructed you to fly to France, didn't he?She asked, shaking her head. 'Why is everything so extreme between you and men?'

'Come on, I'm not going to go,' I explained. I didn't tell her I had looked up flights out of curiosity.

My friends, understandably, felt I was strange for becoming so rapidly fascinated with someone I didn't know. But they were also used to it; finding a new love interest had always felt like a greedy child getting a toy on Christmas Day. I pulled the packing open, became frustrated trying to get it to work, played with it incessantly until it shattered, and then threw the broken shards of plastic in the back of a cupboard on Boxing Day.

I emailed Farly a recording of my and David's original interview.

I wrote, "Listen to this." 'And then you'll understand why I'm behaving so crazy about this guy.' An hour later, I got an email back from her. 'OK, I see why you're behaving so crazy about this dude,' it read.

We spoke on the phone about a week after we began messaging. Everything felt different than when we spoke months ago because the dynamic between interviewer and interviewee had shifted. It was late and quiet, yet I could hear his breathing and crickets in the French countryside. I closed my eyes and could almost feel him next to me; the charm of this odd intimacy we'd developed in the previous week.

'It's nice that we can get to know each other before we meet,' he remarked. 'Shelley Winters once remarked, "Whenever you want to marry someone, go have lunch with his ex-wife."

'Are you recommending that I have lunch with your ex-wife before having lunch with you?'

'No, I just think people offer such an edited sales presentation of themselves on a first date that you don't get to see much of who they truly are.'

'Yes, I believe it will be too late for a sales pitch by the time we meet.'

Another week passed, with thousands of texts and dozens of calls. He grew increasingly fascinating to me, and I was curious about his perspectives on everything. I was fascinated by the hair-splitting nature of our conversation, which spared no detail. He had something new to say about everything that piqued my curiosity. Having the light of this man's interest beam on me left me feeling rejuvenated and new. There weren't enough hours in the day to converse with David. I needed a lot more.

Text messages and phone calls quickly become insufficient. We sent each other all of our work. He sent me unpublished chapters from his new book, and I sent him drafts of articles and screenplays. We told each other things we wouldn't have known if we hadn't talked and looked up pictures: my nails were always bitten down due to my anxiety, and his fingertips were rough from playing guitar. I watched short films in which he appeared with singular focus; I believed he was a genius and told him so, jotting down phrases that stood out to me and shots that I adored and called him later to discuss them.

"Go look at the moon," he urged late one night while we were talking on the phone. I slipped my trainers on and threw a coat over my T-shirt and underwear. I strolled to the end of my street and entered Hampstead Heath. He told me about a wild-haired woman he once dated who lived in Highgate and gave him a thirty-second head start on sprinting into the Heath at night before chasing him down. They had intercourse in the woods, against an oak tree. I sat on a seat at a viewpoint overlooking the city skyline, stretched my bare legs out in the moonlight, and told him about another bench I'd seen here that made me cry when I read the homage carved into it. I spent the entire summer swimming in the meadow next to the Ladies' Pond in memory of Wynn Cornwell, a woman who swam there until she was ninety.

It reads, "In memory of Wynn Cornwell, who swam here for over fifty years, and Vic Cornwell, who waited for her." He must have remained at the gate as she swam every day. Isn't it beautiful?'

"You know..." he began to say.

'What?'

'Nothing,' he replied.

'No, go ahead, tell me.

'You are such an interesting girl. You are this open book in so many ways. Why do you keep saying, "I'm an island"?' he asked.

'I don't aware I'm doing it; it's not a conscious affectation.'

'You might not believe you can have it, but you can. Everything can be yours if you want it.

'I can be moved by something but not know if I want it for myself,' I admitted. 'And I'm just a sap, anyway. It's as if a janitor comes in every year to clean the space between my heart and my tear ducts. One day it will be just one long, clear passage of filthy, pouring emotions, and by the time I'm your age, I'll probably cry at the sight of a leaf in the breeze.

'If you are lucky.'

'The gap between your small faith and the steadfast faith of others can be very touching.'

I don't know. Maybe you just have an unfillable void," he replied with a soothing sigh. 'Maybe no man will ever be able to fill it.' I looked above me at the same side of the moon we were both looking at and wished on a star that I could go to bed that night and forget what he had said.

I was conscious that I was investing a significant amount of time and energy in a complete stranger, but I had every reason to believe him. I counted the days until there was just air between us, and in the meantime, I cherished this haven we had created; he was like a door at the side entry to mundane, daily life, allowing me to slip into a magnificent technicolour world. If I had a difficulty, I turned to him for advice. If I found myself seeking for the finish of a sentence while writing, I would seek his advice.

'Thank you for being more honest with me,' he texted me one afternoon. 'It is sexy.

Obviously, I would continue to do almost anything if a man I liked told me it was sexy.

We frequently discussed how bizarre the intensity of our communication had been to him; it was absolutely new and unusual. I'd never built such a strong bond with someone I'd never met before, but after my formative MSN training and later adult years of online dating, I was more used to speaking with strangers.

'Isn't that weird?' He messaged me, 'You and I have never met, yet look where we've been! The regions of closeness and compassion, Sundays, laughing, and music."

'I understand!'

And we made it all out of unseen energy. Only using pixels.

'We are magicians.'

'See what we're doing with these pixels,' he wrote. "Bouncing each other off satellites."

I scarcely slept the night before David returned to England. He planned to leave his children off at their mother's house, drive to

London, and sleep at a friend's house before our perfect date the next day. The weather was looking excellent; I planned to meet him on Hampstead Heath in the early afternoon with a bottle of wine and two plastic cups. India and Belle assisted me in selecting my clothing, which was a blue tea dress and white plimsolls. I cleaned my flat. I got some nice bread ready for the inevitable morning after.

'She means business,' India remarked as she watched me meticulously remove the volumes off my shelf, clean the ledges, and rearrange the books in the order I imagined he'd find most impressive (Dworkin, Larkin, Eat, Pray, and Love).

But, the night before our scorching afternoon date, I had a date. A matchmaking firm wanted me to write about them in my dating column, so they set me up blindly. It was planned weeks before David and I began our virtual relationship, and it made perfect sense at the time: they needed the publicity, and I needed a date and a copy. I didn't want to disappoint the poor guy, so we planned a very early evening drink somewhere central. I knew I'd be home by nine.

'Call me later, heartbreaker,' were David's final words to me.

I didn't turn out to be a heartbreaker; quite the reverse. We didn't want to be there, as is typical of most situations. He was still in love with his ex-girlfriend, with whom he had unhappily messed things up, whilst I was obsessed with a man I had never met. We shared our respective stories. I advised him to go to his ex's house with flowers and tell her he'd never stopped loving her; he told me to go home and get an early night because I was seeing the man I was clearly going to marry the next day. We departed after one cocktail, took the same tube home, and separated with an embrace.

'GOOD LUCK!' he yelled to me as the tube doors shut between us.

'You, too!' I mouthed through the glass.

When I got home, I called David to tell him about the date. He had traveled down to London earlier than expected and was staying on his friend's sofa in a flat about two miles west of mine.

'Come on, remain here,' I urged.

'How about tomorrow's great date?' he inquired.

'I know, I know, it seems crazy that you're only a ten-minute drive away.'

We agreed to keep to the original plan, and five minutes later, I checked my phone and found a message from him.

'I am coming around.'

I tiptoed out of the flat and down the iron outdoor stairs, and there he was on my quiet street, only the moonlight highlighting his tall, broad shape and the curls of his dark hair. I hesitated on the steps for a little minute to take him in, as if I had jumped off a precipice and was about to hit the calm water's surface. I ran up to him, wrapped my arms around his neck, and we kissed.

'Let me look at this girl,' he murmured, clutching my face and flicking his gaze around my features as if studying me for a test.

'Nice to meet you,' I said.

'Well, it's good to meet you too.' We continued kissing in the middle of my road in the middle of the night, while I stood on my bare toes on the asphalt, with the twit-twoo of a suburban owl in a nearby tree. He drew me in, and I pressed my face against the rumpled navy shirt that matched his curls.

'You're not six feet,' he muttered into my brow.

'Yes, I am,' I answered, standing up taller.

'No you are not, and I knew you weren't, you fucking liar.'

I grabbed his hand and we crept up the stairs to my flat.

The next few hours went just as I had imagined. We drank, spoke, listened to music, lay down close to one other, and kissed. I breathed in his nude, tattooed skin, which was walnut-brown and dusty from the French sun, as well as the fragrance of tobacco and earth. I observed his characteristics that a phone and a photograph could not capture: the curve of his eyelashes, the way an 's' slid between his teeth. He listened to me carefully and spoke to me directly; I felt open and trusting, amazed at my capacity to feel so intimate with someone I barely knew.

'Do you know what's funny?' he asked, kissing my forehead.

'What?'

'You are exactly how I expected you to be. Like the child on the playground who covers her eyes with her hands and believes no one can see her.

What do you mean?

'You cannot hide from me,' he said. I knew I could never lie to this person. I realized I was fucked.

'Are you unhappy that we didn't go on the perfect date first?' I inquired as I slipped into the dreamy, murmuring fallow space between consciousness and sleep.

'No,' he replied, stroking my hair. Not at all. 'What are you doing tomorrow?'

'Meeting with an editor at one,' I announced.

'May I come meet you after?' he said.

I closed my eyes and drifted into a quick, peaceful sleep.

A few hours later, I was awakened by a sound. David stood at the end of my bed, getting ready.

'Are you okay?' I inquired sleepily.

'I'm alright,' he protested.

'Where are you going?'

'Go for a drive.'

I looked at the clock: five a.m.

'What, now?'

'Yes, I'd want to drive.'

'OK,' I replied. 'Do you want me to give you my keys so you can come back inside?'

No, he said. He leaned down on the bed and kissed my arm from elbow to shoulder. 'Get back to sleep.'

He closed the door. I heard him leave the flat, get into his car, and drive away.

I glanced at the white ceiling of my bedroom, attempting to piece together what had occurred. I was overcome with a foul feeling of harsh rejection. I felt it in my stomach and throat: self-disgust, self-loathing, self-pity squared. It was exactly how I felt when I received Harry's call all those years ago.

At seven a.m., I crawled into India's bed and informed her what had happened.

'It sounds like he freaked out,' India replied.

'What about?'

'Perhaps it was suddenly too real. 'Too intimate.

'I mean, the man is an intimacy coach,' I explained. 'That is essentially his job.'

'It could be a matter of "Those who can, do…"'

'I still can't believe what happened,' I said.

'Whatever his motivation, he's got a lot of explaining to do today.'

'But perhaps he will never talk to me again.'

'Certainly not,' she replied. 'He's a father of four; he must have more sympathy than that.

'If I hadn't had the texts on my phone suggesting he was coming over, I'd swear I had a dream last night,' I replied. 'I've been lying awake, torturing myself with these shards of him; his eyes, freckles, and the tattoo on his chest—'

'Oh, of course he has a tattoo on his breast,' India remarked, rolling her eyes. 'What is this?'

I can't. "The irony is too awful."

'Go ahead,' she said.

'Some emblem that represents respect for women.'

'Jesus wept.'

'He should have it updated with a footnote,' I said. 'There's an asterisk next to "Apart from Dolly Alderton."'

'Are you okay?' India inquired, touching my arm. 'This must be a huge shock.'

'I am just bewildered,' I said. Is that it?

A few hours later, David sent me a riddle-like message.

'Hello,' it read. 'Sorry for the awkward exit. It was so beautiful to see and touch you; it sent me very inward, and I felt this abyss between the amazing closeness we've developed in the last few days and the reverse, not "knowing" one other. I watched him type and refused to respond until I received anything that made sense. 'It prompted me to ask some significant questions. Fuck. I hope you're not in pain; perhaps you're just "whatever". But perhaps you are weirded out. I stared at my phone, still unsure how to answer. 'I hope you did not wake up depressed,' he wrote.

'I woke up depressed,' I said. 'I rarely allow people get near to me.'

'I understand. I'm truly sorry. It was not an abandoning of you.

I recalled the last call I had with Harry. I begged him to love me, and I convinced him through tears that I was good enough for him. I listened for any hesitation in his speech that would lead me to feel I could urgently cling to him, my fingers growing purple from the clasp. That was not my tale anymore. That was not who I wanted to be.

'I'm not sure what the above implies, but I'm fine with leaving it here if you don't feel comfortable continuing,' I wrote.

'I need to pause and clear my thoughts when it comes to you,' he said. 'I am not suggesting it should be the end.'

I typed, 'I am'. 'I need to push stop now.'

'Shit, I have hurt you. I can feel it.

'It's okay,' I said. 'We're both going through some weird times in our life. You just got out of a relationship, and I'm going through all of this analysis. But I have to defend myself.

'OK,' he replied.

I removed our talks and call history first, followed by David's phone number.

As the days went, I experienced loneliness, embarrassment, grief, and fury. I felt like an idiot, like a frumpy female character on The Archers who is wooed by a devilish, gorgeous stranger before he leaves with all her money. Friends shared similar embarrassing situations to help me feel better, such as being duped into false intimacy with strangers. One of the editors of my dating column forwarded me an article titled 'Virtual Love' from a 1997 issue of the New Yorker about the bizarre new phenomena of falling in love online; a first-person piece from a female journalist who began a phone and email connection with a stranger. 'I might not have known my suitor,' she wrote. "But, for the first time in my life, I knew the deal: I was a desired person, the object of a blind man's gaze. If we met on the street, we wouldn't recognize each other, our particular version of intimacy now obscured by the branches, bodies, and falling debris that make up the physical world."

Two days after David left me in the middle of the night, the magazine published the article that had first introduced me to him. I'd entirely forgotten about it, but seeing it on the shelves of a newsstand seemed like everything had gone full circle. I didn't text him to let him know it was out, as I had promised in the original message that started this disaster. I never spoke with David again.

My pals were left reeling in the aftermath of the encounter, with the whole affair getting increasingly ludicrous as time passed. Sometimes, weeks and weeks later, we'd be in the pub and India would abruptly drop her glass of wine and say, 'Can you BELIEVE that David guy?' Belle considered reporting him for misusing his position of trust.

'But who could you possibly denounce him to?' I asked.

'There must be some guru council, some kind of equity thing where they qualify,' India stated.

'Maybe we should just contact Haringey Council,' Belle offered. 'Tell them there is a guru at large who poses a threat to naive young women.' Some acquaintances thought he was just a sexist who perceived a woman with trust issues as a challenge, got what he wanted, and then fled, like a wolf in Glastonbury stall-owner's clothing. Others, more gently, believed that he was less at ease with the reality of virtual seduction than a millennial. I was used to talking to strangers and building connections with them. Meeting someone in person for the first time was always awkward, but getting to know someone was just the art of reducing that distance, the 'chasm' he mentioned. That is the entire notion of online dating.

Helen proposed another theory: he was experiencing a midlife crisis as a result of his breakup, and I was nothing more than an impulse purchase for his ego. I was a leather jacket or a fast automobile that he enjoyed the notion of but knew he would never use or fit into his life. However, mourning David's death would be like to a toddler grieving the loss of an invisible friend. Nothing was real. It was speculative; it was fiction. We played intensity chicken with each other, sluts for inflated, false sentiment and a frantic want to feel something deep within ourselves. It was words and spaces. It was pixelated. A Sims-style game about dressing up for love. It was bouncing off satellites in a carefully orchestrated dance.

Only now, after hours of dissection, do I understand who David was. He was not a joker, a living midlife crisis, or a caddish Don Juan dressed in Birkenstocks and linen. He was the small boy on the playground who covered his eyes, believing no one could see him. But I was eventually able to see him since we were two of a kind; kids who were equally awful. He was lost and searching for a lifeboat. He was sad and needed a distraction. We were two lonely persons in need of a fantasy to help us escape. Perhaps, with twenty years on me, he should have known better, but he did not. I hope to never be involved in a game like that again. And I hope he finds what he's searching for.

ENOUGH

In the weeks following my meeting with David, feeling exposed and embarrassed, I made a loud, defensive vow of celibacy. Of course, it wasn't really celibacy because it only lasted around three months. Second, it was primarily a tactic for attracting male attention; a sort of born-again-virgin fantasy challenge. This is the polar opposite of the desired result of celibacy. No nun has ever accepted a vow of celibacy, therefore she appears seductively difficult to obtain.

Then came the catastrophic Christmas special. My pals developed the term 'Christmas Special' to describe a specific type of intoxicated carefree fling that only occurs in the run-up to Christmas, when everyone is high on merriment, goodwill, and advocacy, and all bets are off. In the run-up to Christmas, I decided I'd earned an instant boost of self-esteem.

After a work party, I emailed a guy I'd been conversing with on a dating app for a few weeks, a Geordie working in the music industry with a cheeky face and good chat-up lines.

'Would you like to do our date right now?I messaged him with belligerent nonchalance. It was half-past one in the morning.

'Certainly,' he responded.

He arrived at my flat at 2 a.m. with a bottle of organic red wine. We made small conversation on the sofa as if we were two smart metropolitans on an early evening dinner date, rather than the awful truth of desperation. After exactly one hour of conversation, we began kissing. Then we went to my bedroom and had unremarkable sex. It was the physical equivalent of a hasty meal at a motorway service station: you thought you were looking forward to it, but the moment you got there, you wondered why.

I hadn't slept with a stranger since the night I met Adam in New York. I'd grown out of one-night stands, like a little girl who discovers she no longer wants to play with her Barbies. As soon as it was over, I knew I would never do it again. The intercourse was fine; but, his presence was unpleasant. The illusory intimacy of casual sex, which I used to enjoy as a student, now seemed like a farce. This was not his fault, but I wanted him out of my flat, my room, and my bed, which had letters from my friends on the table beside it and a wonderful memory foam mattress topper that I had saved up for. Seeing the silhouette of this stranger's sleeping face in the darkness made me uneasy. The night went by slowly.

I awoke with a bad hangover, and the Geordie remained in my bed. He wanted to spend the morning lying around together, drinking tea, and listening to Fleetwood Mac records; I was dealing with a 'boyfriend experience' person. The 'boyfriend experience', I had noticed over the years, was something certain men offered after a one-night stand in which they behaved inappropriately romantically the next morning in order to either make you fall in love with them or alleviate their personal feelings of guilt for having sex with someone whose surname they did not know. They spent the morning spooning you, cooking you breakfast, and watching Friends episodes before leaving around twilight. They never phoned back. It was an apparently free service with a significant emotional cost. I never accepted the 'boyfriend experience' when it was offered.

'Have a wonderful life,' I replied as I stood at the door, having finally gotten him out of my house using the ruse of some bogus lunch plans.

'Don't say that,' he replied, hugging me.

'Sorry,' I said, unsure what else to say. 'Merry Christmas.'

I laid on the sofa, wearing Leo's pullover that I had never thrown away, and watched daytime TV. India's darling lover entered the living room, bearded and smiling, wearing the comfortable Fair Isle scarf she had lovingly chosen for him for Christmas. He was a symbol of comfort and love, yet I had never felt so far away from him.

'Good morning, Doll,' he said.

'Nice scarf.'

"Yes, it is, isn't it?'" he murmured, smiling down at it. 'India informed me that you commissioned a Christmas Special last night.'

'Yeah,' I murmured, burying my face in the sofa cushion and peering at the Loose Women panel.

'Good?'

'No. Awful. 'Depressing,' I commented. 'It was an EastEnders Christmas special.'

'Oh dear,' he exclaimed. So there will be no recommission?'

'No. It was a one-off.

My dating column ended the next month, so I no longer had an excuse to be constantly seeking for the next bloke under the premise of it being my career. The end of the column could have easily signaled the start of a new chapter in my life, one free of late-night calls from old boyfriends, right-swiping and left-swiping, cornering men at dinner parties, and coordinating cigarette breaks in the pub when there was an attractive man outside.

The truth was that the column had served as an enabler, but I was the addict. I had always been, long before I became sexually active. Jilly Cooper claims in an edition of Desert Island Discs that when she was in an all-girls school, she was so obsessed with boys that she fantasized about the eighty-year-old man gardener who would occasionally work on the grounds. I was that girl growing up, and in some ways, I've never stopped being that girl. Boys captivated and terrified me in equal measure; I didn't understand them, nor did I want to. Their purpose was to gratify, whereas female friends offered everything else that mattered. It was a method of keeping boys at arm's length.

When Farly and I returned from Sardinia and she embarked on her new life as a single woman for the first time since her early twenties, I delivered an imperious TED lecture on the intricacies of modern dating.

'The first thing you need to grasp,' I continued, 'is that no one meets in person anymore. Farly, things have changed since you were last on the market, and you have no choice but to adapt to them.

'OK,' she replied, nodding and making mental notes.

The good news is that no one genuinely enjoys online dating. We all do it, but everyone dislikes it, so we're all on the same page.

'Right.'

'But don't get offended if you're in a pub or somewhere and aren't being talked up. It's perfectly natural. In reality, occasionally a man will enjoy your appearance at a party but not speak to you, only to later Facebook message you and say he wishes he had spoken to you.

'Weird.'

"Very, but you get used to it." It's just a new approach to establish an initial connection with someone.

What about tit-wanks?' she inquired.

'So what about them?'

Do people still do tit-wanks?'

'No,' I replied authoritatively. 'Nobody has given or received one since 2009. It will never be expected from you.

'That's one good thing, at least,' she added.

Farly met a man in a bar a week later. They swapped numbers. They quickly began seeing each other.

"Farly has met someone," I told India at breakfast on Saturday morning.

'Good for her,' she responded. 'One or two slices of toast?'

'Two. You won't believe where. Guess.'

'I'm not sure,' she replied, nibbling a scoop of lemon curd.

'In a bar.'

What do you mean by "in a bar"?'

"In, like, real life." He approached her and started talking, and they are now dating. Can you believe it? I'm thrilled for her, but also quite angry. I mean, when was the last time you met someone in a bar?'

'How ridiculous!India expressed genuine fury.

'I understand,' I responded. 'I understand.'

Belle schlepped into the kitchen wearing her dressing gown.

'Good morning, kittens,' she replied, sleepily.

Did you hear about this?India inquired indignantly. 'What about Farly's new partner?'

'No?'She answered.

'They met at a bar.'

'What bar?'

'I don't know,' I replied. I believe the name is Richmond. Can you believe it? I don't think anyone has given me their phone number on a night out in around five years, but it happens to her in five minutes.

'Perhaps it's a south of the river thing,' Belle speculated.

'I guess it's a Farly thing,' I replied.

When it comes to love, Farly and I have never been more different. Farly is a comfortable, cohabiting, dedicated, long-term, textbook monogamist. The portion of a relationship that I enjoy the most - the unknown, the high-risk, the exciting first few months when you can barely eat because of butterflies in your stomach - is the part she dislikes the most. Barbecues at a boyfriend's family home, two baked potatoes on the sofa on a Saturday night in front of the television, long automobile rides on motorways together - these are utter joy for her. She would gladly sacrifice the first three months of passion for a lifetime of homemaking, companionship, practical goals, and baked potatoes. I would give anything for a lifetime of those first three months on repeat, as well as the assurance that I would never have to travel to an Ikea, a National Express coach stop, or a relative's home outside of the M25 with a sexual partner.

'Projecting' is one of the treatment terms you learn along the process. It implies accusing someone else of doing or becoming exactly what you fear you are in order to avoid taking responsibility; this is known as 'watch-the-birdie' blaming. I did it a lot when it came to Farly's romantic decisions. I had always viewed my constant refusal to commit as a form of emancipation; I had no idea it was what kept me stuck. Farly may have always felt the need to be in a relationship, but she knew exactly what she wanted. I needed something, but I had no idea what, and I resented myself for wanting it.

Farly and I went for a long walk, and I told her about my plans to take a genuine vacation from sex, including all of the prologues and epilogues of flirting, messaging, dating, and kissing, in order to regain some autonomy. I informed her that, despite being unmarried for the majority of my life, I had realized I hadn't been truly single since I was a teenager. She agreed and told me that it was an excellent idea.

"Do you think I'll ever feel settled with someone?"I asked her as we leaped over logs in Hampstead Heath's trees.

Of course I do. You simply haven't met the appropriate man.

'Yes, but that's the point. I don't think it's about the right man; I believe it's about myself. I suppose the males are kind of irrelevant till I sort all this out.' I waved at myself with tiredness, as if I were a teenager's cluttered bedroom.

'Well, I think it's great you're taking the time to do it. I believe it will be short-term work with a long-term reward.

'Why are you finding it so easy?I asked her. 'I was always jealous of how easy you had it with Scott. You were just there, in, and bang. Committed.'

'I'm not sure, honestly.

'When you were engaged, did you ever consider that you'd never sleep with anybody else? Did it never disturb you?'

'Do you know,' she continued, 'now that you've said it, I don't think I ever thought about it before.'

'That can't be true,' I exclaimed, bouncing like a child as I moved, my fingertips touching a tree branch.

'Honestly - I know it seems strange - but I don't think that thought ever crossed my head,' she admitted. 'I only wanted a future with him.'

'I want to know how it feels to be fully dedicated to someone, rather than having one foot out the door.'

'You are very hard on yourself,' she replied. 'You can have long-term love. "You've done it better than anyone I know."

'How? My longest romance lasted two years and ended when I was twenty-four.'

'I'm talking about you and me,' she explained.

I couldn't stop thinking about Farly's remarks over the next few days; I thought about how we'd known one other for twenty years and how, in all that time, I'd never grown tired of her. I reflected on how I had grown to love her more and more as we grew older and enjoyed more experiences together. I reflected on how happy I am to tell her about good news or ask her perspective on a situation; how she is still my favorite person to go dancing with. Her value increased as we shared more history, like a lovely, precious work of art hanging in my living room. Her love showered me in familiarity, comfort, and tranquility. I had been made to believe that my sexuality was the most important aspect of a relationship, which is why I always behaved like a cartoon nymphomaniac. I never imagined that a man could love me in the same way that my friends love me, or that I could love a man with the same dedication and care that I love them. Maybe I've been in a great marriage all along without realizing it. Perhaps Farly represented what a good relationship felt like.

I poured myself into abstinence like I was pursuing a PhD in it. The more books, articles, and blogs I read on sex and love addiction, the more I knew what I had done wrong. Dating had evolved into a source of quick gratification, an extension of narcissism, with little to do with connecting with another person. I repeatedly mistook intensity with a man for intimacy. A stranger proposed to me at JFK. A middle-aged guru has asked me to go out to France to spend a week with him. It was exaggerated, full of unnecessary emotion, and lacked a strong connection with another person. Intense and intimate. How could I have gotten them all mixed up?

A month had passed, and I felt nothing except complete, unfettered relief. I deleted the dating apps from my phone. I removed the phone numbers I used for booty calls. I stopped responding to ex-boyfriends who messaged me at 3 a.m. asking seemingly casual queries such as 'How's everything doing, m'lady?' or 'What's the problem with Smith?' I stopped hunting possible conquests online, and I deactivated my Facebook account mostly for this reason. I stopped keeping secrets. I stopped at midnight. I dedicated all of my time to my work and my friendships.

Two months have gone. I learned what it was like to attend a wedding and actually observe your friends' weddings, rather than approaching it as an eight-hour meat market. I discovered what it was like to appreciate the wonderful, bell-like sound of a choir singing in church without frantically scanning the pews, examining the fingers of all the guys to see which were single. I learned to enjoy the discussion of the man next to me at dinner, regardless of his marital status; to avoid battling for the attention of the only single man at the table by saying something improper in a somewhat menacing tone reminiscent of Sid James' bawdiness. I saw Leo for the first time in five years at a party and met his new wife; I hugged them both before leaving them alone. Harry got engaged, and I was not angry at all. Adam moved in with a female, and I texted him to congratulate him. Their stories had nothing to do with me any longer; I didn't require their attention. I felt like I was finally jogging down my own road, building my own pace and momentum.

Instead of attempting to grab any man's attention, I sat on tubes and became immersed in my book. I left parties when I wanted to, rather than frantically making circuits of the room till the very end in the chance of finding someone I liked. I didn't attend events just because I knew specific people would be there; I didn't plan random interactions with people I liked. I went dancing with Lauren one night, and instead of looking for a bloke, I stayed in the center of the dance floor for an hour and danced alone, sweating, swaying, spinning, and spinning.

Are you waiting for someone?' a man questioned, dragging me towards him.

'No, she's right here,' I replied, removing his hands off me.

'I never thought I'd use this word in regard to you, and I don't want you to take offense,' Farly stated a few drinks later in the pub. 'But I've found your presence so comforting in recent months.'

When was the last time you saw me calm?' I asked.

'Well, I just haven't,' she said, drinking the last of her vodka tonic and biting on an ice cube. 'Ever. In almost 20 years.

In late spring, I flew to the Orkney Islands twice to write a feature for a travel magazine about solo vacations. I lived above a tavern that overlooked the port of Stromness, and at night, after a beer and a steaming bowl of mussels downstairs, I'd take for a long walk along the coast and gaze up at the enormous open skies - vaster than any sky I'd ever seen.

After a few days of quiet alone with my thoughts, I wandered beneath the stars and down the cobblestone alleys one night, and an idea crept all over me like captivating, brilliant wisteria blooms. I don't need a dazzlingly captivating musician to create a lyric about me. I do not need a guru to teach me things about myself that I believe I do not know. I don't need to cut off all of my hair just because a boy said it would look good on me. I don't have to modify my shape to be worthy of someone's love. I don't need any words, looks, or comments from a man to believe I'm visible and present. I don't need to flee from discomfort and into a male eyeliner. That isn't where I come alive.

Because I am enough. My heart is sufficient. The stories and sentences swirling about in my head are enough. I'm fizzing and bubbling, buzzing and erupting. I'm overheating and burning up. My early-morning hikes and late-night baths are sufficient. My loud laugh in the pub is enough. My shrill whistle, singing in the shower, and double-jointed toes are sufficient. I am a freshly pulled pint with a nice frothy head on it. I am my own universe, galaxy, and solar system. I'm the warm-up act, the main event, and the backup vocalists.

And if this is all there is - just me, the trees, the sky, and the seas - then I know it's enough.

I am enough. I am enough. The words ricocheted through my body, shaking every cell. I felt them, understood them, and they became part of me. The concept accelerated and jumped through my system like a race horse. I called out to the dark sky. I watched my pronouncement fly from star to star, swinging like Tarzan from carbon to carbon. I'm whole and complete. I'll never run out.

And I am more than enough.

(I believe it is referred to as 'a breakthrough'.)

HOMECOMING

There's so much I don't know about love. First and foremost, I have no idea what it feels like to be in a relationship for more than a few years. Sometimes I hear married folks talk about a 'phase' of their relationship as if it lasted longer than my longest relationship. Apparently, this is common. People have described the first ten years of their partnership as 'the honeymoon phase'. My honeymoon phases have typically lasted no more than five minutes. My friends describe their relationship as if it were a living creature that twists, changes, moves, and grows with time. An creature that changes in the same way that two humans who live together do. I'm not sure what it means to foster that third entity. I'm not sure how truly long-term love feels or looks from the inside.

I'm also not sure what it's like to live with someone you love. I'm not sure what it's like to go house looking together and conspiratorially mutter against an estate agent from the loo. I have no idea what it's like to sleepily choreograph my way around someone in the bathroom every morning while we take turns brushing our teeth and showering in a familiar ritual. I have no idea what it's like to know you'll never be able to leave and return home again; your home is right next to you every morning and night.

In reality, I'm not sure what it means to be a true team with a partner; I've never relied on a romantic relationship for support or relaxed into its pace. But I've been in love and lost love, so I understand what it's like to leave and be left. I hope the others will follow one day.

Almost all I know about love I learned via long-term connections with women. Especially those I've lived with at one point or another. I understand what it feels like to know every little detail about someone and delight in that information as if it were an academic subject. When it comes to the girls I've created houses with, I'm like the lady who knows exactly what her spouse would order at every restaurant. I know India does not drink tea, AJ's favorite sandwich is cheese and celery, pastry causes heartburn in Belle, and Fairly prefers her bread cold so the butter spreads but does not melt. AJ requires eight hours of sleep to function, Farly seven, Belle around six, and India can get by on four or five Thatcherites. Carole King's 'So Far Away' serves as Farly's wake-up call, and she enjoys viewing narrative-driven programs on obesity such as Half-Ton Mom and My Son, The Killer Whale. AJ watches ancient Home and Away episodes on YouTube (astonishing) and buys sudoku books to do before bed. Belle does exercise DVDs in her bedroom before going to work and listens to trance music while bathing. India completes jigsaw puzzles in her bedroom and watches Fawlty Towers every weekend. ('I really don't know how she gets the mileage out of it,' Belle once privately said to me. 'There are only twelve episodes.')

I know what it's like to joyfully strap on an oxygen tank and dive deep into a person's idiosyncrasies and flaws, relishing every intriguing moment of revelation. Like the fact that Farly has always slept in a skirt since I've known her. Why does she do this? What's the aim of this? Or the fact that Belle tears her flesh-colored tights off on Friday nights after she gets home from work - is this a sign of her silent wrath against the corporate system, or simply a routine she has learned to enjoy? When AJ gets fatigued, she puts a scarf around her head; this is clearly not cultural appropriation, then what is it? Was she heavily swaddled as an infant, giving her a calm sense of infantilization? India has a comfort blanket, a torn old navy jumper named Nigh Nigh, that she prefers to sleep with. Why does she refer to it as 'he'? And what age was she when she decided it was a boy? In fact, I would love nothing more than to have a literary salon in which all of my favorite friends bring their childhood comfort blankets to the table and debate their gender identities. Believe it or not, I would find that completely compelling.

I know what it's like to set up and run a home together. I understand what a shared economy of trust is; knowing that there will always be someone willing to lend you £50 until payday and that as soon as you repay it, they may need to borrow the same amount from you ('We're like primary school kids constantly swapping sandwiches,' Belle once said of our salaries. 'One week you need my tuna and sweetcorn, the next I want your egg and cress'). I understand the excitement of receiving mail in December and cards with three names on the front that make you feel like a family. I understand the weird sense of security that comes with seeing three surnames on one account while logging into online banking.

I understand how it feels to have an identity that extends beyond you; to be a member of a 'us'. I know what it's like to overhear Farly remark, 'We don't really eat red meat,' to someone across the table, or Lauren say, 'That's our favorite Van Morrison record,' to a person she's talking to at a party. I understand how surprisingly nice that feels.

I understand what it's like to go through a negative event and transform it into common mythology. We do the same thing with our own micro-disasters as the couple who theatrically tells the story of their bags getting lost on their last vacation, taking turns telling it. For example, when India, Belle, and I moved house, everything that could have gone wrong did. The reality was misplaced keys, borrowing money from friends, staying on couches, and putting things in storage. This is an excellent story.

I understand what it's like to love someone and accept that you can't change certain aspects of them; Lauren is a grammatical pedant, Belle is messy, Sabrina's emails are endless, AJ will never respond to me, and Farly is often moody when tired or hungry. And I know how liberating it is to be loved and accepted despite my shortcomings.

I understand what it's like to watch someone you care about recite a narrative you've heard five thousand times in front of a captivated audience. I understand what it's like for that person (Lauren) to embellish it more flamboyantly each time ('it happened at eleven' becomes 'so this was around four a.m.'; 'I was sitting on a plastic chair' becomes 'and I'm on this sort of chaise longue hand-crafted from glass'). I know what it's like to love someone so much that this doesn't bother you at all; to let them sing this well-rehearsed song and maybe even step in with the supportive high-hat to help the story move along when they need it.

I understand how it feels to be at a crisis point in a relationship. When you think about it, we either tackle the problem and strive to fix it, or we go our separate ways. I know what it's like to agree to meet in a bar on the South Bank, start bristly, and end three hours later, weeping in each other's arms and promising never to make the same mistakes again.

I understand what it's like to feel like you've always had a lighthouse - lighthouses - to guide you back to solid land; to feel the warmth of its beam as it squeezes your hand while standing next to you at a funeral for someone you loved. Or to follow its flash across a packed room at a dreadful party where your ex-boyfriend and his new wife unexpectedly arrived; the flash that screams Let's buy chips and take the night bus home.

I understand that love can be loud and exuberant. It may be dancing in marshy muck and pouring rain at a festival, yelling 'YOU ARE FUCKING AMAZING' over the music. It's introducing them to your coworkers at a work function and feeling proud as they make people laugh and make you appear lovable simply by being liked by them. It's laugh till you wheeze. It's waking up in a country none of you has visited before. It's skinny dipping at morning. It's walking down the street with someone on a Saturday night and feeling like the entire city is yours. It's a massive, gorgeous, and energetic force of nature.

I also know that love is a subtle thing. It's lying on the sofa drinking coffee and talking about where you're going to drink more coffee in the morning. It is the process of folding down pages of books that you believe they will be interested in. It's hanging up their laundry as they leave the house because they forgot to take it out of the washer. It says, 'You're safer here than in a car, you're more likely to die in one of your Fitness First Body Pump classes than in the next hour,' as they hyperventilate on an easyJet flight to Dublin. The texts are: 'Hope today goes well' and 'How did today go?', 'Thinking about you today', and 'Picked up loo roll'. I understand that love comes beneath the beauty of the moon, stars, fireworks, and sunsets, but it also happens while you're laying on blow-up air beds in your childhood bedroom, sitting in A&E, in line for a passport, or stuck in traffic. Love is a peaceful, soothing, relaxing, pottering, pedantic, harmonious hum;

something you may easily forget exists, despite the fact that its fingers are outstretched beneath you in case you fall.

I had been living with my pals for five years before it ended. Farly had left me for her lover, AJ had left, and India had called me one day to say she was ready to do the same, before breaking down in sobs.

Why are you crying?I asked her. Is this because of how I treated Farly when she met Scott? Were you afraid I would go insane? Do you all think I'm nuts? That was about four years ago; I'm more suited to handle this now.

'No, no,' she sniffled. 'I am just going to miss you.'

'I understand,' I responded. 'I'll miss you too. But you turn thirty this year. And it's wonderful that your partnership is ready to move forward. It's perfectly natural for things to change.' I was taken aback by my own logical reasoning and silently awarded myself a CBE for services to friendship.

What are you going to do?' she inquired. 'You've always expressed a desire to explore living independently.'

I don't know. I'm not sure if I'm ready for it,' I added. Perhaps I should live with Belle until she decides to move in with her guy. It gives me at least six months to figure out what to do next.

'Dolly, you're not in the Hunger Games,' she said. 'It shouldn't be an endurance challenge among our friends to see who can stick with you the longest.'

I understood I'd been presented with an opportunity. I could wait until all of my pals had met a man and moved out. I could rent from strangers on Gumtree who kept shaving cream in the fridge in the hopes that I'd eventually find a man and move out. Or I could begin a new story on my own.

Finding a one-bedroom flat to rent within my budget was difficult; I was shown a lot of properties with mattresses next to ovens and showerheads poised over a lavatory in a 'wet room'. There was the'spacious one-bed' that was twenty square meters in size, and there was one with police tape around the front door. India accompanied me to viewings, negotiating and interrogating the bluster of estate agents, and asking whether I truly believed I could live without a closet and instead store all of my clothing in a suitcase beneath the bed.

But eventually, I found a home in the heart of Camden that was reasonably priced. It was a ground-floor unit with a bedroom, bathroom, and living room, as well as enough area for a closet and a shower that hung over a bathtub. At the back, there was a sunken, wet kitchen with no drawers and a porthole window that made me feel like I was on a boat. It wasn't ideal, but it would be mine.

All of us who had lived together went on a 'farewell flat-sharing' pub crawl in our twenty-something neighborhood. We arrived dressed as elements of flat-sharing in our twenties, which was just as bizarre as it sounds. AJ arrived as Gordon, our first landlord, complete with a midlife crisis leather biker jacket, white trainers, a short brown wig, and a persistent smarmy grin. Farly, the resident obsessive cleaner, showed up dressed as a huge Henry vacuum in a spherical suit with a pipe connected that dragged around the ground as she drank. Belle arrived as our loud nightmare neighbor, wearing smudged lipstick and a Cher wig. India arrived as a large bin, as emptying, relining, and taking one out seemed to be the most common theme of our time together, with bin liners tied around her shoes, a lid for a cap, empty face wipes, and Monster Munch packets clinging to her body. I arrived as a massive packet of cigarettes and quickly regretted it as people approached me and asked for free cigarettes, figuring I was some sort of Marlboro Lights promotional model banging the streets of Kentish Town.

We went from pub to pub before coming back outside our first yellow-brick house. We even stopped in on Ivan at the corner shop, only to learn from his coworker that he had inexplicably 'gone away for some unfinished business' and vanished 'without a trace'.

'The artists have left,' Belle murmured regretfully as we went around the crescent, day becoming to dusk. 'Now the bankers will move in.'

A week later, I taped my potted plants and paperbacks into cardboard boxes for my new home. On our final night together, India, Belle, and I drank discounted Prosecco - the cocktail of a bloody decade - and danced drunkenly to Paul Simon in our empty living room. As we waited for our various moving vehicles the next morning, we huddled in a corner of our wine-stained carpet, our knees knocking together as we sat side by side, speaking little.

Farly, the most efficient and organized person I've ever met, came over to help me start unpacking the day I moved into my new house ('Are you sure you want to do this?' I texted her; 'Please - this is like cocaine to me,' she replied). We ordered Vietnamese cuisine and sat on my living room floor, slurping pho and dipping summer rolls in sriracha sauce, discussing where we should put the sofa, chairs, lights, and shelving, as well as where I would sit and write each day. We unloaded late into the night before falling asleep on my mattress propped up against the bedroom wall, surrounded by cardboard shoe boxes, clothing bags, and book stacks.

When I awoke, Farly had already left for work, and there was a letter on the pillow in her plump childlike handwriting, which hadn't altered since she put notes on my lever-arch files in Tipp-Ex during science GCSE lectures. 'I love your new home and I love you,' it stated.

The morning sun rushed into my bedroom, leaving a dazzling white puddle on my mattress. I stretched out diagonally over my bed's chilly sheet. I was utterly alone, but I've never felt safer. It wasn't the bricks I'd managed to rent or the roof over my head that I was most thankful for. I was carrying my home on my back like a snail. The feeling that I was finally in capable and caring hands.

Love was present in my empty bed. It was built up in the albums Lauren had purchased me when we were teenagers. It was among the smudged recipe cards from my mother, nestled between the pages of cookbooks in my kitchen cottage. Love was in the bottle of gin tied with a ribbon that India had packed for me, as well as the smeary photo-strips with curled corners that would end up on my refrigerator. It was in the note on the pillow next to me, which I would roll up and store in the shoebox with all of the other notes she had written previously.

I awoke safely in my one-woman boat. I was sailing toward a new horizon, floating in a sea of love.

There it was. Who knew? It was there all along.

Printed in Dunstable, United Kingdom

63510758R00097